HOLLAND

Toledo-Lucas County Public Library

TOLEDO-LUCAS COUNTY PUBLIC LIBRARY

R7ZUX   HOLLAND

JF
Rabe, Berniece.   AUG 0 5 1988
Rehearsal for the bigtime.
#1652545

REHEARSAL
FOR
THE
BIGTIME

BERNIECE
RABE

Rehearsal FOR THE Bigtime

Franklin Watts New York London Toronto Sydney 1988

Library of Congress Cataloging in Publication Data

Rabe, Berniece.
Rehearsal for the bigtime.

Summary: Eleven-year-old Margo, who has always been thought of as nothing more than a sweet little angel, gains confidence and the ability to make people admire her when she joins the school band and starts special music lessons with three friends.
[1. Musicians—Fiction. 2. Bands (Music)—Fiction.
3. Self-perception—Fiction] I. Title.
PZ7.R105Re 1988   [Fic]   87-21636
ISBN 0-531-10504-0

Copyright © 1988 by Berniece Rabe
All Rights Reserved
Printed in the United States of America
6 5 4 3 2 1

For Rebecca Rabe

REHEARSAL
FOR
THE
BIGTIME

CHAPTER ONE

Margo was very willing to rise straight to the top. She wanted to be number one, hit it big, just once in her life.

"Mother, I've thought up some really super costumes for your ballet group," she said.

In spite of the fact—or maybe because of the fact—that she had a keen imagination and could think up much better things than her mother could, she got no answer. She tried putting it another way. "All the little kids would be dressed in different shades of blue and go swirling around and around, and they'd be the waves on the lake. Of course, they'd have to stay onstage all the time. Maybe I could be a monster that lifted its head out of the lake, and—"

"Look, Muffy"—her family called her Muffy, Example A of what she had to tolerate—"Muffy, we're not running a Halloween parade. This is serious theater."

Margo accepted that rejection. She said, "I've got something fabulous that would win top honors at the school science fair. Sixth graders are allowed to enter this year. It's a sure-fire project. Grandfather could help me."

"Discard that idea, Muffy, if you're thinking what I think you're thinking. It'd be an imposition. If you really want to do something, get a project that you can manage by yourself."

Margo was about to wail that Grandfather always wanted to help her do things but never in the way she wanted to be helped. But she refrained. She had more substance than people gave her credit for. Being eleven years old, blond, blue-eyed, and petite can be a terrible burden. Very few people realized that.

People, however, gave applause readily to her older brother for already being a star athlete at twelve. Her younger sister was dramatic and had a keen wit that people were fast to notice. The best Margo got was, "You're such a cute child"—and she was eleven! Or Mother would say, "Be serious." She *was* serious.

She really would have enjoyed being a monster and scaring people with her ugliness. Then they'd have seen how talented she really was. Her science idea would have impressed the entire family. It was time for the world to know that she was something more than fluff. But

Mother was right: It had to be something she could manage by herself.

Her kid sister came trooping by singing "Dumb Dog" while looking at Margo. It was unmistakable that she was Little Orphan Annie. Mother smiled and handed her her schoolbag, and she left for school happy.

"Muffy, dear, if your room is clean, you'd better be off to school, too."

"I fed the hamster. Everyone in this family would let it starve to death if it weren't for me. I'll clean my room when I come home from school." She grabbed her book bag and ran. She didn't even allow herself time to get lunch money from the lunch-money dish. Now she'd have to starve.

Starvation won her considerable attention and an apple from Leroy. And half of a sandwich from shy Helena. In appreciation, Margo went along with both of them to hear Miss Preston demonstrate musical instruments. All sixth graders who were interested could go. Until the lunch sharing, Margo had not been interested.

"You're all at the right age to begin playing an instrument. You may take one home for a two-week trial and approval. Then you and your parents can make up your minds which instruments, if any, you wish to purchase. There is an installment plan. Be sure to tell your parents that, please.

Stop fooling around and listen now, so you can choose an instrument if you've not made your decision already."

Margo sat as still as possible and listened. And thought.

If she took the drums and cymbals, she could really be heard. But they were not her style. She wanted an instrument that was *her*. The violin sounded wonderful the way Miss Preston played it. But then Ernestine demonstrated how very well she, too, could play it. She had been taking private lessons on the violin for over a year already.

Ernestine whispered to Margo so Miss Preston couldn't hear, "Hey pickle, don't take the violin. Choose the piccolo!"

"I never planned to take the violin."

Who in her right mind would want to be shown up by Ernestine Niles? Ernestine was tall and dark, and no one ever called her cute or fluff. She was as hard as steel, as in a crooked nail. She always got heard. She always got her way. If the class was to take a trip, it was Ernestine's plan that got accepted. She'd already started a project for the science fair. Everyone in school had listened while she told how she planned to get tomatoes to survive on nothing but air and water. Ernestine would probably be the only sixth grader to enter.

Margo hated her.

At the end of the instrument demonstration,

Margo said to Miss Preston, "I'd like to take the clarinet home. It's perfect. It's not too high and sweet like the piccolo, and it'll be easy to hide."

"Margo, why on earth would you want to hide it?"

"I share a room with my kid sister, who is six. Hiding my possessions is a real necessity. If you knew her, you'd understand."

She certainly didn't plan to share her clarinet with her sister. There was too much sharing going on as it was. Mother included both of them in the ballet classes she taught. Already her sister was so good, she was destined to become a star. That was reason enough for Margo to bow out, to take her swan song and go on to sounds—and plenty of them. Music would be her own thing.

She hummed all the way home, trying to make clarinet-type sounds. When she got home, she explained everything—almost—to her mother. She didn't tell her that taking a musical instrument was a matter of choice. What she called out on entering the door was, "We have two weeks before we have to start paying for my clarinet. I'm going to be in the school band."

Maybe her mother didn't hear her, for she didn't act shocked or interested. She just nodded as she dashed by and said, "Fine." Mother was putting something in the oven with one hand. In her other hand was a pair of half-mended tights, the thread dangling from the needle. On afternoons when Mother was scheduled to teach ballet, Margo had to try a little harder to make her listen.

So while her mother continued her flitting about picking up and cleaning up, Margo unpacked the clarinet from its beautiful case, fitted the mouthpiece on, and began. That is, she tried to begin. She puffed and snorted. She hummed and gurgled. What humiliation! What pain! Ernestine barely touched bow to violin string, and music came forth. But even Ernestine had had to begin at one time. Every last musician alive—or dead, for that matter—had had to begin sometime, somewhere. Margo told herself that and puffed another enormous puff.

BRUMPF! FRUMF! UMP!

Mother sailed past her and went into the laundry and started the washer. She stayed in there, Margo was sure, until three loads of wash were done. No use alibiing for Mother; she must be hiding from Margo's sounds.

When Margo finally stopped trying to make notes come out instead of those strange sounds, Mother emerged with an armload of folded laundry. "Whatever was that awful racket? I thought I told you, no TV until homework was—" She let some of the laundry topple on the floor in her astonishment. "What have we here?"

"My clarinet." Margo smiled broadly and figured she'd excuse Mother after all. She'd caught her on a bad day and at a bad time. Then she raised the clarinet to her mouth and said, "Just listen!"

Her brother came bursting through the door just then, one jump ahead of her father. "Anybody seen my shin guards?" he demanded.

"You're home! I put the shin guards in the closet where they belong. Oh dear, I've lost track of time again. Margo, grab your sister and let's run." Mother was gathering up dance bags and heading for the car. She shouted back at Father, "You two guys can eat the left-over roast. It's sitting in the microwave ready to heat. Margo has something to show you both later. Good-bye, good-bye." She blew kisses. Margo's little sister was right there mimicking Mother.

Margo said, "I'm not going. I have to practice my music."

That got Father's attention. But while he was inquiring about the clarinet, Mother was yelling that Margo must hurry or they really would have to leave without her. Margo never hurried, and Mother and little sister left without her.

"Here, let me show you how it works," Margo told Father and blew into the mouthpiece. Out came a big BRUMPF! FRUMF!

Father gave a sharp grimace, which he followed with a big forced smile. He said, "Hey, Muffy, that's real nice! Look, your brother's found his shin guards. We have to leave for the soccer game. You just keep tooting away, and we'll be back before you know it."

"Tooting" was not a nice way to describe a musician's work, but Margo realized she was not a musician yet. One day, he'd no longer use that term.

Her brother left last. "Don't blow so hard, Muffy. And try to make something other than that awful racket, or you'll make us all deaf."

"No sound comes out unless I blow real hard."

"Well, I can tell you right now, Father will never buy that horn if you can't play it right. Maybe you'd do better if you got a piccolo."

Margo seethed to think it was the same suggestion she'd gotten from Ernestine. "I don't want a piccolo! Father *will* buy this clarinet. You'll see and he'll see just how great I'll be on it by the time you get home." Then Margo saw Father coming back to hustle her brother out and added, "Anyway, the interest on the installments is tax deductible." For emphasis she gave a shake of her long golden tresses.

Her father was a tax lawyer and always heard the word *deductible*. He was also an avid photographer, and he melted when she acted cute and swung her hair about. He would consent to buying the clarinet. She knew that even before he said, "You look like a little angel standing there

16—

with her horn, Muffy." He smiled sweetly and was off.

She hated herself for having won that way.

The album on the coffee table was full of her angel pictures—pictures of her in a pink tutu and gossamer wings with toes pointed. Being cute was an awful habit, and she had to break it. She didn't want to get the clarinet on those terms. She was glad her father had to rush away just then.

In the first place, she was beginning to doubt that she'd ever be able to make anything but horrible sounds come from her clarinet. Her brother was probably right. Second, she wanted to be heard because she was doing something well. She wanted people to know she had some substance to her. One look in the mirror, and she saw that the clarinet was indeed a dumb choice. It did make her look like the angel pictures.

But she would not take it back. It was the instrument she had wanted most, and she was going to keep it. She was going to learn to make music so beautiful that her talent would be noticed—not her hair, her eyes, or her size.

CHAPTER TWO

*B*ut Margo had to face some facts before she could make beautiful music on her clarinet.

Fact number one, Margo stated aloud: "I'm not making heavenly music. This is noise and I need help." She went straight to her room and made a sign.

> *I am looking for a qualified listener for a beginning musician during practice time. You must have good ears that can tolerate noise and sharp ears that can tell when the music finally comes. Call Margo at 666-8643.*

She walked the four blocks to Misty's house and taped the poster onto her front door. Misty used to be their baby-sitter before Margo's brother had turned twelve. She was fair and honest and didn't take guff from anyone. When she spoke, even Margo's brother listened. Margo had always wanted to be like her. She didn't know why it had never occurred to her before that the way to accomplish that was through music. Maybe one day she, too, would be a member of the Dundee Scots Marching Band and play a mean clarinet, as Misty did her French horn, while high-stepping along in kilts and tassels.

Fact number two: Any kid who got Misty to lend a listening ear would be the luckiest kid in town. She'd probably charge a fortune, but whatever she asked would be worth it. Margo had three dollars and twenty-eight cents saved. That would be good for starters.

Her parents might pay if she could convince them that it was a necessity, that all the other kids were hiring listeners. Or that the idea had come from an adult and not herself, someone who was respected and spoke with authority. She'd like to mention Misty to Father as soon as he got home, but it'd be wiser to wait for the agreement of some respected adult.

It was just as well, since Father returned home in a sour mood. Her brother's soccer team, which Father coached, had lost. He complained, "Some tax problems are worse than a challenge. The Bentons are getting very old, and their records aren't complete. I've got to go over and pick up some more of their papers even if my mind is on that roast beef. And Muffy, honey, I'll have to listen to you play that horn a little later."

His regular business was with a big oil company, but on the side he did the Bentons' taxes. Margo understood that he did this moonlighting to provide them with the little extras in life. He often said that. Maybe now was the time to mention Misty after all.

"I'll go with you," she offered. That brought a smile to his face.

As they rode along, she forgot Misty for a while and just enjoyed the fact that there was no one in the car but Father and her. He was a smart man and a good man, and she loved him a lot. When she did think of Misty again, she was smart enough not to mention it just then and spoil the mood. But who knew when the right time might arise to sway Father to her way of thinking about hiring a professional listener? She'd do it in a straightforward way, too. She'd not cuddle up to him or act cute, even once.

Father said, "The maid always hands me the papers at the door. What I need most is a chance to get inside and talk to the old couple themselves. Drat it. I, who can get Arabs to negotiate, can't get that maid to hear a word of any argument I have to offer. She reminds me too much of my mother."

"I know just how you feel," said Margo. She liked it when Father talked to her in this adult way.

At the Bentons' she was surprised to see a red-haired boy her own age sitting in a chair under the great carport puffing into a tuba. Father had to stop short so he wouldn't hit him.

While Father collected the papers from the maid, Margo said to the boy, "Hi. You just beginning?"

"You can tell, huh?"

"I never saw you in sixth grade? You got an instrument to try out?"

"Yeah. I'm in sixth grade at St. Andrew's. This is my great-grandfather's tuba. I have to learn to play it, but I'm having trouble. You having trouble, too?"

"Not me. I'm hiring an expert professional listener. You wouldn't be interested, would you?" She told him all Misty's qualifications.

He kept nodding and nodding, so she had him sign a paper for her to show Misty that he was serious. Actually, she planned to show the paper to her father when the right time came.

"My great-grandfather Benton is hard of hearing, and he wants me to get really good on this tuba. He'll be happy to take me to a qualified listener for practice. He knows I already get enough teaching. It's just that he's no good at listening to me practice."

Margo felt she'd wait until that fact was confirmed. Then she'd tell Father that the Bentons had this wonderful idea to get a listener for Peter and produce the signed paper. Next, she'd ask for the same privilege. She waved a friendly good-bye to Peter.

Father noticed, but he was mumbling that the heap of jumbled tax records was too much. He didn't comment about Peter.

Misty called that night to say she was interested in the job—very interested. She was a sophomore in high school, too young for most well-paying work because of the laws, so she welcomed something other than baby-sitting. She was happy to hear that Peter would come along, too.

"But Margo, I'll take you only on the condition that you come up with two more students, for a total of four. And things will be on my terms. I'll listen to one student for one hour each day. That will take care of four days. You'll each pay two dollars for your day. Then there'll be a group listening for everybody on Friday. The charge will be two dollars from each of you that day, which means on Fridays I'll get eight dollars. That's still a bargain, because I am the best."

It sounded fair to Margo.

"It's a deal. I'll keep my ears open."

The next day at school, Miss Preston took tall, lanky Leroy gently to one side. Margo listened while Miss Preston explained to Leroy that he would not be able to master the trumpet since he could hear only from one ear. "One needs two ears for the direction of sound. Drums require only a sense of rhythm. Perhaps you'd like to take a drum home to show your father."

Margo liked Leroy because he was smart, because he seemed to like her, and because he'd given her an apple to save her from starvation. Leroy's problem couldn't be much different than Peter's great-grandfather, who had trouble hearing. She told Leroy not to worry because Misty could be his listener. She really laid it on thick about Misty being the best. Leroy, being a whiz at math, calculated the odds that such a plan would work. He said no to the trumpet and to Margo and took the drumsticks home. Margo wished she could return his old apple that she'd eaten.

    Defeat is never established by one failure, Margo told herself, as her father had often told her, and she went on with her pursuit of clients. It so happened that Helena, the shyest girl in the entire school, who sat next to Leroy during lunchtime and had shared her sandwich with Margo, had overheard. She was taller than Margo but pale and wore two black braids always. She was a great listener while Margo explained things in detail. No comment followed, but none was expected right away, since Helena seldom talked. Her mother talked for her.

Later that night, Helena's mother called Margo's father and asked who he had hired to listen to his daughter practice.

    The call came just after Margo had made

many interesting loud sounds with her clarinet. Mother had already settled three quarrels over whether the rest of the family had to sit quiet and listen or if they could turn on the TV to drown out Margo's noise.

Father put down the phone and shook his head in disbelief. Then he said Helena's mother had finished their conversation with, "My husband and I don't know a thing about music. We don't want our daughter growing up as ignorant as we are."

He asked Margo to explain what was going on.

This wasn't exactly the way Margo had planned to break the news about Misty becoming her listener. But why not take advantage of the moment? "I talked with Misty on the phone last night about how I wanted to spare my family pain when I practiced."

"Right on!" shouted her brother.

"It's worse than pain, it's ruining my life!" said her dramatic kid sister.

"Mother even washed clothes yesterday that were already clean so she wouldn't have to listen to me," Margo added.

"Margo, I never!" Mother was shocked.

Father laughed and slapped Margo on the shoulder in the same way he slapped her brother when he'd made a good pass in soccer. "Um, well, I guess we don't want our daughter growing up ignorant about music, either. You say Misty came up with this listening idea? She's a first-class musician herself."

"The best," answered Margo, making no comment at all on whose idea it had really been. Let Father think what he wished. How beautifully it was all going!

The next day put the frosting on. Leroy came to school saying his father wanted him to have a listener while he played the drums. His father worked hard as a plumber with blowtorches and drills and jackhammers, and he really liked peace and quiet in the evenings. If Misty was the best, then he wanted the best for his son, too. "A boy without a mother deserves to have a woman listen to him once in a while," Leroy's father had said.

That sounded great to Leroy and to Margo. Helena even nodded her approval. Now all they had to do was call up Peter and have them all meet at Misty's to get their days assigned.

Mother had said she would take Margo to Misty's, but Father insisted. Margo knew he liked the idea, but she suspected the real reason he postponed three very important business appointments was to teach his family to spend their money wisely. Father just loved to manage the family budget. What he said was, "I want to make sure that you get there and all things are settled in good order."

"You're not going to argue about the price, are you, Father?" Margo pleaded, afraid Father might spoil this perfect setup.

"You let me handle that. I just want the best for my little angel."

There went the little-angel routine again.

As they went flying out the door and bounded into the car, Mother's last words were, "And hang the cost! Don't give that young woman one moment of controversy over money! We all know Misty's the best at whatever she attempts. Besides, this is important to the sanity of our entire family—especially mine."

"And mine!" shouted Margo's kid sister. "Her noise curdles my blood."

Margo chose not to listen to that statement, and Father also ignored it as they sped off.

When all four cars pulled up at Misty's house, the adults got out to talk. Soon other cars stopped to investigate. They asked if someone was having a garage sale; it was that time of year. It took a lot of pushing and shoving by the parents to convince the outsiders that no such thing was happening. Misty opened her front door with some difficulty.

"Margo, I knew you were a go-getter, but this is too many!"

Margo was flattered that Misty thought so highly of her. Still, she tried to explain.

Misty wasn't hearing any better than the garage-sale shoppers. Misty shouted, "There'll have to be some elimination! If you'll consider my restrictions, some of you may choose to leave. First, I cannot tolerate tardiness for any reason, and my practice hour is set. If any of you had in mind to ask for some hour other than 4 P.M. for your music practice, I am sorry."

There was some protest that there was nothing for sale and more unnecessary shoving, but finally everyone but Margo, friends, and parents were cleared away.

Misty nodded approval; then she stood by the open door, straight and beautiful in her lime green blouse and pants, and ushered them in. Her hair made a soft, misty halo about her head. But no one of her posture and self-confidence would ever be called cute. Margo was filled with admiration.

"That's more like it," Misty said. "I've weighed what sort of work I should do to earn the income I feel I need to make. A job itself should be a pleasure. I love nothing better than to see beginners turn into fine musicians."

Father's jaw, set and ready for argument about costs, dropped. Margo was glad he had the presence of mind to keep silent.

"Well," said Misty. "Now, let me talk to just

the kids. Please. Parents go wait in the family room."

A frown creased Father's face. He was more used to giving orders than to taking them. He stepped back with a quickly whispered word. "Sweetheart, be as agreeable as possible about the cost, unless of course you're cornered."

It wasn't the first time he'd let Margo bargain for herself. He'd done it once at a flea market and once at a school auction. Margo had enjoyed those times. People often said Margo got her coloring from her father. After those bargaining times, Mother added that she got a lot more than looks from her father.

Anyway, when the kids were separated from the adults, Misty began. "All right, you kids, I know that you're unskilled, unlearned, uninformed, unenlightened, and inexperienced."

It took Margo a moment to catch up with the words to determine if she were cornered or not. She finally realized what Misty meant, put simply, was that they were all green.

Misty's next words were, "I know how you must feel. I was once just as unskilled and ignorant as you."

That did it for Margo. She wouldn't allow anyone—not even Misty, who was the best—to call her ignorant. That she considered being cornered.

"I'm not dumb!" she shouted loud enough

to be heard. But just in case Misty didn't hear, she narrowed her blue eyes and moved in close.

"I didn't say you were, Margo," answered Misty, and she gave them all a little lecture on how ignorance wasn't a thing to be ashamed of and how the brightest person in the world is ignorant of many things. Often music. She ended the lecture by saying, "I've earned my way by sweat and hard work, and I will expect the same of you. Now, tell me why you chose the instruments that you did."

Peter said he wanted to please his great-grandfather Benton by being the third Peter to play the tuba. Leroy explained about his hearing loss and how the only thing left for him was drums. Helena whispered that her mother thought a flute would be best.

When it was Margo's turn, she said, "I love the look of a clarinet. I love its long, thin shape and how it feels when I put my lips to the mouthpiece. I loved its sound when our music teacher demonstrated it. I loved the box it came in." At that, everyone, even Misty, laughed. But Margo took it. She didn't feel she was cornered. She felt they had heard her and understood.

Next, the parents (in Peter's case, great-grandparents) were brought back into the room to tell their reasons for hiring Misty. All the reasons were totally acceptable to Misty. Then she posed what Margo had been dreading: cost.

Father was going to be impossible. Margo felt it coming. It wasn't that they were poor; he just loved judging family purchases from all angles.

"My listening fee is two dollars per individual practice hour." Most heads nodded. Father's didn't, but Margo could tell by his face and posture that he didn't object.

"The fee for Friday's group practice hour will be two dollars per person, also."

"Objection!" shouted Margo's father. "A group fee should always be less than an individual fee."

Misty gave him a questioning look and stated, "Usually, but not always. You'll get your money's worth. I am the best."

Father simply said, "Strike what I said from the record. My child stays."

Margo would have died to have her own words heard without argument. And to have a nod of agreement so fast!

Misty shook hands with each kid and welcomed all of them to begin rehearsal for the bigtime. With due consideration, she assigned each a day. Leroy, the mathematician and snare drum player, got Monday. Red-haired Peter would practice his great-grandfather's tuba on Tuesday. Shy Helena, who would play the flute and who'd likely have to sit behind Ernestine and her violin, got Wednesday. When Margo had seen the existing school band seated, she had been very glad she'd chosen the clarinet. It was not so close to the violins.

That left Thursday for Margo. "I thought maybe I was disqualified 'cause my father spoke out," she said.

"Not at all. You were already chosen before I even called you. I expect great things from you, Margo."

"Me, too," said her father. "Glad you came up with this idea, Misty."

Margo groaned and ran toward the car so her father would hurry and not have time for a reply.

Maybe part of her groan was because her plan was working too well. Could she live up to such great expectations? Did she really have any talents worth developing? She'd made nothing but noise so far. Whatever—she was in this too deep to back out now.

So she went home and made more of the gosh-awfulest sounds ever heard to come from a clarinet. Nothing to compare to the sweet music of Ernestine Niles's violin—yet!

CHAPTER THREE

On Thursday, Margo was at Misty's at exactly one minute before four. She understood that Misty had meant it when she had said, "Be on time."

The door opened, and there was Misty with a huge smile and a happy spark in her eye. "Margo, come in. Ready for your first day of rehearsal for the bigtime? Come into the family room. I want us near the kitchen. Sometime in the future I may be cooking as I listen. Or I may do laundry chores or an experiment—or whatever. Here, this is your chair."

Margo took the small armless chair with its carved and curved legs and beautiful needlepoint seat cover.

Giving Margo her absolute complete attention, Misty said, "All right. Begin."

Margo felt as shy as Helena. Anyone would feel shy when they know they're the worst and someone is sitting there waiting to hear every mistake. Maybe she didn't want to be heard after all. She looked down and polished her clarinet with the tail of her blouse.

"Begin. This is costing your parents two dollars an hour. Don't you want your father to get his money's worth?" There was fire in Misty's eyes. They scorched Margo into beginning.

She blew her own anger into her clarinet, not caring anymore how she sounded. *Puff. Puff. Splutter. Spit.* No sound came out. She couldn't do this. She was cute. She didn't have to be heard. No, no—she wanted to become number one. Again she tried, harder and harder, and . . . and then the sounds came loud and fierce.

"Hey, you did it! Listen to that volume! Oh Margo, you are going to be good! You'll reach the top balcony. One expects volume from a tuba, but from a clarinet? Do it again."

Misty had heard! So Margo did it again a few hundred times.

Misty seemed ecstatic. "The greatest miracle is a kid making living sounds come from inanimate metal and plastic!"

"But it's not music," said Margo, feeling just a little uncomfortable because she was being applauded only for the amount of noise she could make.

"Music will come later. You won't recognize

change when it happens unless you can hear it. Right?"

That answer surprised Margo a bit, but after a while it seemed sensible. At home the moment she'd made the first sound come, she guessed she'd felt ecstatic, even if no one else had.

The more Misty applauded, the more Margo made those sounds roll out. That hour was shot in a hurry. It had flown!

When Margo got home, Mother asked, "Well, how was practice?"

"Fine, I guess," answered Margo, careful not to show too much enthusiasm. Her parents might think she wasn't getting anything out of what they were paying for if she acted too happy.

"Is that all?"

"Nothing to talk about."

"You're a strange one, Muffy. First you accuse us of not listening when you want to talk. Next you say you've nothing to talk about. Well, you're going back next time. We've made a commitment and we must stick to it. This is for your own good."

Margo turned her face toward the window so her mother couldn't see and smiled. "Okay, I'll go," she said.

On Friday all four—Peter, Helena, Leroy, and Margo—were at Misty's at one minute till four.

34—

"Welcome! Come in. Come in. Come in. Come in!"

After everybody had been greeted and Peter, who was from private school, got introduced, they took their assigned chairs. Then the noise began and it grew and grew until the entire neighborhood must have heard it. Then Misty called, "Halt! Stop the racket!"

For a moment Misty almost sounded like Margo's parents. But then she said, "Those were the most odious, offensive, disgustingly wonderful sounds I have ever heard. You'll all become winners! Today you are the worst. You've got nowhere to go but up. By the final recital, you'll be the best."

"Better than Ernestine?" asked Margo.

"Of course. You'll be the tops."

With great zest and zeal, Margo led in and the rest followed. After ten minutes, even Helena forgot her shyness. The noise began to grow and grow and swell and swell and reverberate around the room. Squeaking and squawking. Tweedling and twanging. Rat-a-tat-tats and moanings like a dying calf. It was a glorious uproar, a hullabaloo of a rumpus. Margo felt that at last she was being heard.

In a *bad* way, of course. So bad, in fact, that Misty had to remove Leroy's drumsticks from his hands and throw herself over Peter's tuba to get them to hear her. "Stop the racket!"

Margo put down her clarinet. Helena put down her flute.

"You kids hardly have harmony, but you sure have *dis*harmony down pat. You're terribly loud, and that's good. I can't stand a kid who's afraid to let those sounds come out. I think we'll be able to hear those musical notes when they come."

"Absolutely."

"Emphatically."

"You betcha."

"I guess you're right, Misty," said Helena, since everyone was waiting for her comment, too.

"You're a fine gang, but your practice time is up. It may not be easy on your parents this weekend, but I want you to practice every day. They'll be rewarded when you're being praised later. Build up your lungs and muscles. Get used to your own noises. Next time I'll expect you to hear musical notes. Don't let anything or anybody stop you. I'll see you next week."

The children put their instruments into their cases carefully and ran outside. Well, Peter didn't run. He could barely move his tuba. His old and bent great-grandfather was there to meet him, and between the two they managed quite nicely. Peter got into his great-grandfather's long black Cadillac, Leroy got into the cab of his dad's pickup, and Helena sat very close to her mother in their little compact car. They might be the worst

36—

musicians in the world, but they were all Margo's friends.

"Misty said we sounded horrible," Margo volunteered to Mother when she got home.

"Well, you'll go back as we planned. Give this thing a little time. We're paying plenty for that instrument. I'm sure your father would want you to stick with it for a while."

"I'll try," said Margo.

"Good girl," said Mother, and she patted Margo's knee.

It was all so wonderful. Margo had never had a plan work out so well in her entire life.

The next session Misty asked them to listen to silence. Then she had them make as low a sound as they possibly could. She shushed them, hushed them, threatened to put a muzzle on them if they didn't tone things down a bit. No more scratch and scrape, toot and hoot, rasp and blast! The time had come for them to listen for music. They listened hard but found none.

On the following Thursday during Margo's private listening session, Margo finally heard music. Delight swept over her. Now she would be heard in a good way. Misty had heard, too, for her entire face, mouth, eyes, and eyebrows seemed astonished. She whispered, "Music! I heard a musical note just then. Do that note again."

Margo did. And then she did another perfect note and played it over a dozen times. In all, she discovered eight. Misty leaned back in her listening chair and said, "Talent. I knew you had it."

Perfect! What was even more perfect was that all four of them had talent. Misty said so and she wasn't given to idle flattery. Within six weeks they were playing little tunes like "Twinkle Twinkle Little Star." And not long after, when Misty tossed out such words as *tone, pitch, key,* or even *timbre* on group practice day, they all knew exactly what she was talking about.

Margo and her friends were growing in confidence, as suited Margo's plans. She felt sure now that she could build a strong new personality around something other than her looks. That is, as long as she had Misty to applaud her.

Misty had gotten a school calendar and had had a talk with their music teacher. She studied it while they watched. She lifted her head and used the word *recital.* The others gasped. Margo's blood ran cold. The recital was to be on a school day, and there'd be no Misty there. It was Helena who argued, "We can only make music when you listen, Misty."

"Yeah," said Margo. "Even you said we were the worst. My mother still makes me practice in the garage. That recital will be full of kids who are the best. Ernestine, who's had a full year of private lessons, will be there to show off."

"You're good enough by now, too, to be heard and appreciated by others," declared Misty. "At each recital, you'll be better and better. You'll catch up with and overtake Ernestine. Do what I say and I promise it."

At that statement, Margo took hope and argued no more against the recital. Leroy began to calculate how much they would have to improve at each recital to accomplish the feat of overtaking the best players. "I'd say we need to go to a hundred and ten percent to outdo them. We've probably already got fifteen percent learned. That leaves a ninety-five percent gain still needed. That'll mean another fifteen percent this recital, thirty a couple of times, and then a twenty percent gain on the last recital to go over the top. Do you think it's possible?"

"It sounds scarier than ever the way Leroy puts it," said Helena.

"It sounds dumb the way Leroy puts it," said Margo. "Why didn't you just divide ninety-five by four?"

"Things usually go with a big burst at first and then slow down a bit at the top point," explained Leroy. He watched lots of television and was real smart.

"Hm-m-m-m, I couldn't have put it better myself," Misty declared, and Leroy beamed.

What Margo liked most about Misty was that she was fair. She even gave praise when a kid was smarter than she. Margo had seen a lot of adults struggle with that. She gave Leroy approval by slapping him on the back. Then Misty looked toward Peter.

"Peter, I've asked permission for you to come to the recital with your friends. It's all okayed."

"I have a snake who will have babies about that time. I doubt that I can be at the recital."

"That does it!" said Margo. "That excuse takes the cake." She got very serious and made her eyes flash mean and green. "You will be going to the recital or you'll not have Misty for a listener again."

Misty didn't contradict her, so that was that. They'd all be going to the recital. Ernestine would be there with her violin, but who cared? It was too painful for Margo to think about what would happen if she herself were shown up. And if she dared show Helena up, Margo thought she'd kill Ernestine.

CHAPTER FOUR

*T*he sky was dark and dank, a miserable sight, as Margo stomped through the mud on the way to school the day before the first recital. Ernestine had boasted to their class how she would be the star of the show. Indeed, their school music teacher, Miss Preston, had assigned Ernestine a small solo part, even in this first recital.

Of course, she meant this to offer encouragement to a promising young student. But what did it offer to Margo and her friends? Discouragement. Rejection. Jealousy, envy, indignation. Resentment, anger, and a hard clenched fist—that's what!

If Ernestine was star material, then Margo was the President of the United States.

Margo shivered. What if they didn't make the fifteen percent gain in excellence at this recital? If Ernestine was even one-hundredth as good as she claimed, it would be tough going.

Margo had some mean, nasty thoughts. She wanted to hide Ernestine's violin during recess or pass around a note that said, *Don't you think Ernestine's music stinks? Yes. No. Circle only one.* But she couldn't do that sort of thing. She'd confront Ernestine. Head on.

Well, it so happened that Ernestine set herself up. The whole school was out on the playground with a skeleton crew of teachers standing guard. The other teachers took a long-needed rest to devour a platter of brownies in the teachers' lounge to replenish their strength. No kid was supposed to come back inside during recess unless there was a dire emergency—like dashing into the bathroom. But Margo saw Ernestine walk casually back inside the school. Margo followed.

Sure enough, Ernestine sneaked into the music room and when Margo came through the door, she had her hand one inch from Margo's clarinet. "Lay one finger on that instrument and you die!" Margo threatened in the deepest, meanest voice she could muster. Since Margo was the smallest girl in the class she had to fight with words, not her fists. To be impressive now, she doubled her fists.

It scared Ernestine plenty. She didn't even withdraw her outstretched hand. It hung there in midair.

"Start saying your prayers," said Margo.

"If I should die before I wake," began Ernestine.

"If you should die before the bell, Ernestine Niles, you'd go to . . ." Margo had no intention of finishing that sentence. She always stopped short of saying a bad word. In this case she couldn't have finished, for at that instant their music teacher walked in.

"What's going on in here?" demanded Miss Preston, licking the final bit of a nice chewy brownie from her finger. "Do either of you have permission?"

Silence.

Margo realized that not only she but Ernestine, too, had enough smarts not to talk when a teacher had been aroused from her well-earned rest. Anything said would only increase the tension in the atmosphere.

"I'm waiting," said Miss Preston.

Silence.

"All right, so that's the way you two wish to play the game. Ernestine, there'll be no solo part in the recital. Margo, it'll take some time to think up your punishment. You're already in the last chair. I'll talk to you later. At least it's good to see you two on friendly terms. Now back outside, both of you."

In the hallway, Margo took shadow jabs at Ernestine's midsection, not hitting and not intending to. She just wanted her not to think they were friends. "If you're a star, I'm the President of the United States."

"At least I know I'm not considered one of the worst musicians in the world!" Ernestine knew how to rub things in.

They met the kids coming in from recess, so they didn't actually have to obey Miss Preston. Margo quickly told Leroy to recalculate their odds for a fifteen percent gain of excellence in the recital. She had managed to get Ernestine denied a solo. Of course, goodness knew what she herself was in for.

The bell shrilled right above Margo as she was asking Leroy about their other problem: "Did Peter's snake have her babies yet?"

Leroy lived close to Peter and the two had become friends since they'd met at Misty's place. "Naw," said Leroy. "The snake'll probably have 'em right at recital time. Peter planned to skip school in the afternoon, anyway, to be in our recital. I think his folks arranged for it."

"Babies or no, he'll have to come. A snake doesn't have to be watched, for heaven's sake!"

"Of course not, but Peter wants to watch. And he does just about everything he wants to do. Sometimes his great-grandparents say no to him, but he just pretends he doesn't hear them. He says, 'Turnabout is fair play.' They don't hear him most of the time. I don't have it so lucky. My dad hears *everything.*"

"My dad, too. And I never win an argument with him." Margo liked finding she had a lot in common with a boy. She had absolutely nothing in common with her brother.

"Yeah, my dad says your dad can argue like a Philadelphia lawyer."

"He's worse than that," explained Margo. "He's a tax lawyer right here in Houston."

"Gee. How about that? You going to be a tax lawyer someday?"

Margo really loved that. No one had ever asked her that in her whole life. "I might," she answered. "Hey, I guess I will. And my practice for it will begin right now. I've got to see Miss Preston and argue my case. Why should I live in dread of her punishment when I'm entirely innocent?"

"Miss Preston," began Margo, "this is my very first recital in all my life and I guess I'm nervous. When I saw Ernestine coming inside, I came in, too." Miss Preston didn't appear much affected by that story. Then Margo dropped her head so her long blond hair swept low and covered her face and said, "I just don't want to quit."

Margo hated herself for winning with cuteness instead of a good, sound argument. But she even overdid the cuteness. Miss Preston not only agreed to make allowances for Margo's nervousness and drop all charges, but in order to be fair, dropped all charges against Ernestine as well. What had all this gotten Margo? She'd just blown their fifteen percent gain, that's all.

She went to Misty's for practice. Misty refused to listen to her complain. Misty just made her get on with her music. "Your parents are not paying me two dollars to listen to you *talk*. Now practice! This is no cheap-shot recital *even* if it is just before the students at school. This is rehearsal for the bigtime, which is where you're headed, Margo. Maybe I am the only one who knows it right now, but soon you will know it, and after that others will know it. Play!"

Margo had no choice. Toward the end she thought that perhaps she was getting good, that maybe she was becoming a person with some skills. Maybe she'd even be able to perform tomorrow in the presence of Ernestine. But, oh, poor Helena! She had to sit right beside Ernestine.

Leroy called her on the phone the minute she got home from practice. It was the first time a boy had called her. She'd called a couple of boys herself, but that didn't count.

"I need your help, Margo. Is there any way you can come over here and help me persuade Peter that he's got to go to the recital with us?

Our group has to be represented one hundred percent."

Margo was still thinking about being a lawyer. "Well, Leroy, it'll be a hard case, but I'll see if I can talk my father into bringing me over. Go ahead, count on it. I've been practicing the art of argument today."

It was easy. The minute Father knew where she wanted to go, he started backing out the car to take her. "For years I've wanted to meet the Bentons casually, win their cooperation. Besides, I'd like to get a look inside the house," he said.

Peter's great-grandparents' home was near the bayou on a hill with a deep front lawn. Margo took note of that. In case it ever snowed again in Houston, as it had two years ago, she planned to go there immediately.

The mansion had once looked out over vast acres. Now there were many other beautiful homes around, one sitting right next to the other, just like Margo's home sat close to their neighbor's. She wondered if Peter let his snake play in that grass.

It was not exactly a grass snake that Peter had. Father hinted at and got them the grand tour of the house, which ended in the area where Peter kept his boa.

"Where the heck did he get that snake?" Father asked.

"He brought it with him on the plane. Had

47—

it wrapped around his chest under his shirt so his mother wouldn't know." Peter's great-grandfather laughed in sort of a brittle, cackling way. "Neither did we, of course. He took the boa through the detector at the airport gate and all the way home before we knew. He's a chip off the old block, sure enough." Margo's father laughed, too. Margo wasn't laughing. She'd hate to be on a plane and have a snake get loose.

After hearing all that, Margo didn't know if she could talk Peter into doing something he didn't wish to do. However, she had promised Leroy and she'd never gone back on a promise. Besides, it was for the sake of their group. No one else played a tuba. The tuba would make it a smashing show for them. She guessed she'd better do it—better do it right now.

"Peter, you absolutely must show up at the recital tomorrow. You've made a commitment. Honor it!" She tried to sound just like Misty and she didn't miss the mark by much.

All of a sudden, Peter's great-grandfather's head jerked high and his back seemed to straighten. He said, "Peter, you are our guest until Christmas and a most welcome one at that. We have tried to permit you every pleasure. We have even arranged for good housing for your boa. But there is one thing I cannot allow, and that is for any Benton to go back on a commitment. Rest assured, young lady, that Peter will be at the recital."

When Peter's great-grandfather talked like that, he didn't look old at all.

"Yes, sir. I hear you, sir," said Peter.

So all four of the gang were there for the recital. Peter whispered as he slipped into his chair, "She had her babies this morning—I watched it all. Ten! I brought one along to show you." He pulled the baby snake out of his pocket.

That put all four of them in a festive mood, so they played really loud. Helena was shy at first, but Margo poked her a few times with the bell of her clarinet. Then Helena stood up and played so loud that you could hardly hear Ernestine at all. Of course, Ernestine got heard quite clearly during her solo. She acted like a star and all that. But who cared? Just as she sat down, Peter was taking his baby snake out of his pocket to check its welfare. Ernestine pointed at Peter and screamed, "Snake! Snake!" Then she screeched and screeched until her eyes bugged out.

Peter started to put the snake back into his pocket, but students pushing for a look threw Peter's aim off, and the snake landed in his tuba instead of his pocket. It headed down inside into the dark. Margo felt sorry for Peter, who loved that snake and was trying to take care of it.

"Where is the snake, Ernestine?" asked Miss Preston, a bit annoyed.

"P-P-Peter's p-p-pocket?"

"Peter, do you have a snake in your pocket?" asked Miss Preston.

"No, ma'am," answered Peter politely. "See?" And he pulled out his pocket linings to show they were empty.

After everybody finally got settled, Peter quietly retrieved his little pet and put it safely back into his pocket. He stood up and played, sat down and played, took bows after playing like all the rest, and the recital was over.

The applause was wild because people had had a good show before they had to leave to catch buses and whatnot. Everything had been accomplished quite quickly and satisfactorily.

Since the recital had fallen on a Friday, Margo and her friends went together to Misty's for practice.

"Were you good?" asked Misty.

"We were the loudest."

"Great, but did you earn the fifteen percent gain? Did you give them a good show?"

"We did that," stated Leroy. "No doubt about it."

No one mentioned the snake. There had been no agreement, but they all just knew not to mention that part of their act. Misty had told them before that music belongs in all of life. If all of life should be touched by music, the snake had already had its share. But they were the only ones who needed to know that.

"Well, why didn't you shout it out? This demands a celebration! All achievements must be celebrated. Let's see, what can we do to celebrate? I'd like to give you a cast party. That would be the appropriate thing."

"Brownies and punch, maybe?" asked Peter. "At home I have to eat Spanish garlic shrimp with Greek salad and Jewish challah bread. And for dessert we get German Black Forest cherry cake or, if it's a light dessert day, French pears in red sauce or English trifle. But never, never, never do I get brownies and punch."

"Sorry," said Misty, "I don't have time to make them. We can't go over the hour I've scheduled for listening."

"Then why don't we plan for a celebration on another day? You can sit and listen while we plan." Margo was no fool. She liked to stay within rules but she, too, believed in never missing out on a party.

"You're a genius!" shouted Misty. "And I know just what you can plan. All celebrations do not have to be with food. Some can be just a special shared activity. I heard of a neat one today! One of my uncles is our precinct captain, and the other is running for mayor over in Conroe. I often hear them swapping plans on how to build up community pride. I usually know what's going to happen around here way in advance.

"Right now I'm going to tell you so you can get a head start and take the grand prize. Big money! You just have to promise me one thing— that you'll use music in it. Your parents are paying me two dollars an hour to listen to your music. I can't stray too far from that responsibility, even if you have had adequate practice for today. But I will consent to listen to you talk about using music."

Margo knew that Misty wasn't trying to stretch her job. She was just practicing what she proclaimed: music should be used in every phase of life.

Margo joined with her friends in a huddle around Misty to hear the great advance announcement. And when she heard it, she began to applaud and ideas started flying around in her head. Thoughts were swirling about, stirring the air, filling her heart and lungs. It's hard to explain that sort of excitement except to say if notes were attached to it, it would have been a great symphony.

CHAPTER FIVE

What Misty had gotten wind of was an upcoming parade at the end of October. It would be announced in the papers in a week or so. It was to be unusual in that it was a group competition. The theme would be books. The group was to dress up as characters from a book of their choice. The city fathers had felt it would add a new flair to the usual Halloween parades, whose purpose was to keep kids in their own neighborhoods and to cut down on their time for trick-or-treating.

Margo had always loved dressing up and making up for the Halloween parade. It was more than just being seen for one's cuteness. It told the world of your imagination and talent. Best of all she got to look ugly. She'd be the best monster anyone ever saw.

First they had to send in a card of intent with the name of the book they'd chosen. In all of

Houston, no two groups could choose the same book. The neighborhood parades were scheduled to start at five and end at six, and any trick-or-treating that followed was to end by seven. That left two hours to sort, count, divide, and eat candy before going to bed at a decent hour. However, the top winners from the neighborhoods would parade in downtown Houston at the witching hour, midnight.

Misty said, "The minimum number per competing group is three and the maximum number ten. The minimum age is five; the maximum age twelve. You four would make a perfect group. So choose your book."

"Think of a really scary book," insisted Margo.

"Does it have to be a scary book?" asked Helena.

"No. Any fiction book. Adult, kids. Doesn't matter. But try to keep in mind the costumes and my rule that you must take along your instruments and make music for the parade."

"You're right," said Margo. "Every Halloween parade I've seen has been a silent one. But the scariest movies always have some scary music. Okay, let's start brainstorming about the book. Which one lets us use the scariest background music?"

Margo picked up her clarinet and made a scary sound come out of it. Maybe it wasn't music like they played at school, but it was the sort that movie makers have used for a long time. "Isn't music wonderful? It can make you feel scared or sad or loving or whatever." Margo was so intent on her discoveries that she missed her share of the brainstorming and the others agreed on a book.

They settled on *King Arthur and His Round Table*. Peter wanted to be the king. No amount of arguing on Margo's part could change anyone's mind. She finally stopped arguing when she remembered that her father had once made her brother up as Merlin the Magician for a school play. Merlin was from that book. Her brother had gotten scads of applause for doing Merlin, even though his acting was terrible. She'd like to be a better Merlin than her brother. "My father studied stage makeup in college," she told the others.

"Why did a lawyer study that?" asked Leroy.

"He thought any good lawyer could use a few courses in drama, and makeup was included. He says he'll never do any acting except in the courtroom. But he's always willing to do our makeup. He does all of us every time Mother gives a dance recital. Or when it's Halloween. Or he does himself when he plays Santa at Christmas, or when he wants to scare the living daylights out of Grandma."

Helena declared, "I'd like to be Merlin."

"But I wanted to be Merlin. I need to show

my brother I can be a better Merlin than he. I had that idea in the first place—that's why I agreed to your old book."

"You can play Guinevere," said Leroy. Then he asked Helena, "Why do you want to play Merlin?"

"Because if I'm magic, I won't be shy," said Helena.

Margo thought Helena wasn't all that shy right now insisting on a part that she wanted. "Okay, be Merlin. I'll be King Arthur. All I need is some padding and a beard," said Margo, defying Peter.

Peter said, "I said from the beginning that I was the king, and I'm going to be the king!"

Leroy punched Margo playfully in the stomach. "Peter gets to be King Arthur because he is the roundest. You can be Guinevere."

Peter said, "Padding and a beard would just make you look like a pregnant man. Yeah, you be Guinevere." He settled back, knowing he'd gotten the part he wanted.

Leroy said, "I'm a knight. I insist." No one objected, so he, too, settled back. "Well, Margo, are you going to be Guinevere or not?"

"Why should I be?"

"Because you look the part."

"Big deal! What good is costuming if you look the part?" She could have cried. Her very own friends were doing this to her—calling on her cuteness.

She agreed at last by remembering how Father always did their makeup. He could apply his skills to someone else better than to himself. Well, she would make her troupe the winners. It was a chance to use her talents, and she couldn't spend forever arguing with them. Helena would be a better Merlin than her brother had been; she'd see to it.

When Misty clapped her hands like cymbals and shouted, "Time's up," their plans were settled, and they were ready to leave for home.

Actually, Peter hesitated. But Misty insisted that he leave on time. She would allow no violation of her rules—no tardiness, no staying late. So, once outside, Peter got his snake out of his pocket and, looking at it, told Margo his problem. "How am I going to march in a parade with a big costume on and carry my great-grandfather's tuba, too?"

Margo thought a minute, then whispered a good answer into his ear and they both went happily on their way. She'd rather be the director of an event anytime than eat brownies and drink punch.

Her father was home when she got there. He came home early on evenings when Mother left to teach ballet. "Well, Muffy, how'd the recital go today?"

"We were a sensation. Kids were saying it was the best recital they'd ever attended."

"Misty's that good, huh? I thought so from that first day."

"Father, I'm going to make up our music group for a Halloween parade. Peter's King Arthur, Leroy's a knight, Helena's Merlin, and I'm Guinevere."

"Of course you're royalty. You look the part. I won't even have to put makeup on you, princess."

Margo scrunched down. Father hadn't even heard her say that she was going to do the makeup. Also, he'd been happy she was cast as Guinevere. What can a kid do when the whole world's got her typecast? She made a decision right then and there that by the time this parade was over she wasn't going to be typecast anymore.

For the next two weeks the gang practiced the songs they had decided to play during the parade, individually and together. Misty often worked in the kitchen now while listening. "She made brownies on my day," boasted Peter as he brought out a sample from his pocket that he'd saved to share with the rest.

Leroy said, "On my day she restrung her tennis racket."

"On my day she punched holes in a stack of papers so they'd go into a notebook," said Helena.

"On my day she made Chinese food—sweet and sour pork. But never did she miss a sour note if I made one." Margo laughed as if she'd said something really funny. Then out of loyalty she added, "But she also said nice things when I did something very well."

At the end of group practice, Misty said nice things again. "By the fall recital, you kids will be doing great. Playing during that parade will get you used to playing in front of people other than school friends. It should be a sweep, and you'll make your thirty percent gain. I'm sure of it."

They'd done fine on the signing up for the parade. With their early knowledge, they were able to tear the entry blank out of the paper the minute it arrived and mail it back within the hour. They got dibs on King Arthur and his Court!

Things went sailing along like that for a while. Then at the eleventh hour thunder and lightning commenced. First, Margo's father announced that he had to make a trip to the Middle East to settle some tax issues for his oil company. She was sort of depending on him as a backup just in case she needed help. Of course, he'd thought it was the other way around, and he said now, "I'm as sorry as I can be, Muffy. I wouldn't have missed helping you with makeup and seeing you in that parade for the world."

Margo hated the way adults said they wouldn't miss something for the world, then, like Father, chose to miss it for Saudi Arabia.

Next, Peter was late for his practice, and Misty expelled him!

They could still go on with the parade since the minimum entrance was three, but Peter was their friend. Besides, Peter fit the part of King Arthur. Margo hated herself for thinking like that since she'd resented them saying she fit her part. But Misty refused to let the rest of the group discuss the issue with her. "You're here to practice. Let's hear some music. Peter is a good kid, but if any kid cannot show up for practice on time, he does not have the makings of a winner. I wouldn't even want to encourage him to rehearse for the bigtime. He'll never make it."

Next Leroy got the chicken pox, a disease he should have gotten in kindergarten. But he had to get it in sixth grade. His father said he'd be allowed to go out as soon as the fever was gone and scabs were formed, but who would want to look at a scabby knight? And how could Margo orchestrate things—like seeing if his costume was correct—with him in quarantine? She couldn't even get near him!

Worse, they needed their last-minute practice. Last-minute practices are what put the polish on things. The whole world knows that.

And even worse than that, Margo was angry with Misty. Miss Authority! Tough as nails with her old rules! The very things Margo once respected in Misty now made her angry. She just had to get Peter back into their group. She wished he went to Fairview School so they would have all day to talk this thing out.

At five-fifteen on Wednesday, Peter phoned Margo. This made the second time a boy had called her. "Margo, I need your help. I need to talk to you. All night long I've been saying to myself that Misty is a creep, but it doesn't make me feel any better. Besides, she's not. She made those brownies just because of me." His voice broke.

"Yeah, I know," said Margo. "I guess there is a heart under there somewhere if we can get to it. Why were you late, Peter?"

"It was the maid's day off—it's always the maid's day off on Tuesday, the day I go for practice. I'd have pointed that out the day of the first interview but my great-grandparents didn't want to make waves. Their hearing is bad and they were desperate, so they told me not to worry. They'd always get me there on time.

"But this Tuesday they were late. I could have walked over if I'd known they were going to stay away so long. But I was afraid I'd upset them if they came home and found me missing. They're *very* old, you know. My grandma is afraid they're too old for me to stay with them. So they try real hard to do everything right. They really want me here. Not a lot of people really want me. They say they do, but they don't. If my great-grandfather had found me missing, he might have had a heart attack." His voice broke again. Then he managed to choke out another sentence. "I was afraid they might be dead—in an accident or something. I couldn't leave."

Margo was too choked up to answer. She had no great-grandparents, but she'd feel the same way even if it were her grandparents. "Peter, we've got to make Misty listen to your explanation. I know she'd let you come back if she would only listen. Ha! She gets paid for listening to music, but she won't even listen to something as serious as this! I hate anyone who thinks kids are just something to see and never listens to what they have to say. I hate her!"

"I don't, Margo. I really don't. But you're right, we've got to make her listen. That's why I called you. You have the best ideas."

Margo nearly swooned at that. Her pulse was throbbing, her heart was fluttering. Someone was admiring her for something other than her cute blond looks. Wow! The feeling was sensational!

"It's simple, Peter." She was trying to stop the rush of her words and sound all nice and calm and lawyerlike. "We will write to Misty. We will not be present, so she needn't fear she's losing her authority over us."

Margo paused. She'd just quoted Father, who sometimes said Mother shouted because she was afraid of losing authority over Margo. "Peter, you know no one ever leaves a personal letter unopened. We've also got curiosity on our side."

"You're a genius!" said Peter.

"I know," said Margo.

"I'll write the letter myself, and right away," said Peter. "Misty doesn't know my handwriting and besides I'll use calligraphy. Great-grandfather taught me that."

"Great—she'll really die of curiosity."

"And Margo, don't worry. I'll be at the parade. Great-grandmother says Misty can't bar me from that. This parade is for the city of Houston, and Great-grandmother has plenty of pull with the city. I've got a nifty costume. I'll see you there."

"Your letter will work, and you'll see us all at group practice this Friday. You can also tell Misty in that letter that I'll trade practice days with you. Tell her this will never happen again, that the maid will be there to chauffeur you. Oh, and be at my house at four o'clock prompt, so I can check your costume."

When they hung up, Margo was feeling mighty proud of herself. She felt much older than eleven. People always thought she was nine. Looks and size don't mean a heck of a lot, she thought. It's what you can do that counts.

Her brain was still working in high gear, so the next thing she did was call Leroy. The quarantine wouldn't keep him from talking on the phone.

"Leroy, are you feeling well enough for us to discuss your costume?"

"Yeah, sure. I'm up and around. Even went outside today. By tomorrow, I could go back to school if I didn't look so awful. My costume's all I've been thinking about all day. I covered my football shoulder pads with aluminum foil already."

"What for?"

"It looks a little like armor. I've got a long-sleeved gray sweat shirt I could wear underneath, and . . ."

"I got a better idea. My mother has a solid sequined dress—very fancy and very old. It's got a miniskirt. It'd look just like a coat of armor on you."

"Think it'd be all right if we used it? Your mom wouldn't mind?"

"Not at all. It's old," said Margo, with only the slightest of pauses. She knew her mother *would* mind—if she found out.

She woke up next morning with the issue of Leroy's chicken-pocked face solved. She called him at once. His father wasn't too happy about that since it was only five-thirty. But Leroy was really happy with Margo's suggestion: to wrap his football helmet in silver foil, as he'd done with the shoulder pads. Then he could make the foil swoop up into a point at the top like a knight's. Next, wrap the face guard in foil, making it bigger and bringing it to a point like those solid face guards the knights wore. She ended with, "I'll see you at my house tomorrow for a last-minute check. Four o'clock prompt."

"Roger!" said Leroy, who had never been late for anything in his life.

Her own costume was a snap. There are always princesses in ballets, and her mother had a trunkful of costumes for her to choose from. All she had to do was use some poster board and roll up a long pointed hat. She attached one of Mother's long silk scarves at the end.

Helena had gotten permission to come directly home from school with Margo. It was her first time to go home with a friend, and Helena's mother was very pleased. Margo's brother's Merlin costume almost fit Helena, who was considerably taller than Margo. They managed to get her braids up under her pointed hat. "Now for your makeup," said Margo, rubbing her hands in anticipation.

It turned out fabulously! Remarkably well for an eleven-year-old girl who people thought was only nine. It was a distinctive job with her own brand of pizzazz to it, a makeup job that might even have impressed her father. Mother took pictures. Her brother never said a word.

Peter and his great-grandparents showed up extra early. Peter was wearing a magnificent velvet cape and a ruffled shirt with a kingly band streaming across the front of it. He also wore some velvet pants that he said were actually knickers that his great-grandfather had worn years before. All the stuff had belonged to his great-grandfather, even the puffy round hat, on which his great-grandmother had asked the maid to sew some huge beads.

Margo found a nice beard from Father's assortment in the makeup kit. Mother helped her glue it on Peter, while his great-grandparents nodded approval. "You look quite acceptable, Peter Benton the Fourth," said his great-grandfather as they took him for the parade lineup.

Mother left for other chores.

"Here comes Leroy." Helena could hardly speak for all the wax and other makeup on her face. "Hurry, Leroy!"

Quickly Margo pulled the sequined mini-dress over Leroy's shirt and stuffed the curvy top section up under the shoulder pads so it draped a little at the neck. From her mother's closet Margo got the silver lamé pants which her mother kept but never wore. They looked terrific on Leroy as he ran out and jumped into his father's pickup. The words "Smith and Son, Plumbing" flashed past as they zoomed away to the parade.

Mother came back inside and asked, "Just *what* was that boy wearing?"

It was a stupendously successful parade. The air was brisk, just right when people are wearing heavy costumes, and the crowd was generous with whoops and hollers. Mostly they whooped and hollered about Peter, for there he was all decked out as a king playing a huge tuba that rested on a round coffee table on wheels. That had been Margo's suggestion. A string around Leroy's waist pulled the table along nicely as he marched as a silver drum-playing knight directly in front of the king.

Helena, with wizardy, flowing robes and stars splashed all over her costume, seemed to spin real magic with that flute of hers. A star attached to the end of it made it look like a magic wand.

Margo floated along, letting the breeze move the folds of her gown and the long silk scarf at the top of her hat, while she made enchanting music on her clarinet. Occasionally, she stopped to blow a kiss, playing her part to the hilt. She'd had much practice at such things in her life. The crowd loved it. It made her rather sick, but the show must go on.

Maybe they sounded so wonderful because they had no musical competition. But they had plenty of competition as far as costumes went. Just about every horror story and scary book that was ever written was represented. *The Monster Family, The Ghoulies,* and *Psycho.* Ernestine came as Snow White, surrounded by her seven dwarfs—the witch would have been a more fitting part. But no one but Margo and her friends had music.

Suddenly, there was Misty marching backwards right in front of them! In their amazement, they stopped playing.

"You kids are wonderful. Just listen to the crowd! You look, uh—ravishing, Margo. You, too, Knight Leroy. Is that you, Helena, oh Mighty Wizard? Peter—I mean, King Peter—I got your letter. I want you back. Will you come?"

"Yes, ma'am. I will," said Peter, and he gave a big blast on his tuba, which was the signal to all to start playing again.

The crowd was nothing compared to the one that cheered them on at midnight in downtown Houston. A boisterous, frenzied, unrestrained lot they were. And that was tame compared to their actions when Margo and crew won the grand prize of two hundred and fifty dollars!

"That'll be $62.50 apiece!" shouted Leroy instantly.

Everyone's parents were proud and stood right beside their kids and right next to the mayor while news cameras flashed.

Leroy stripped off his costume, then quickly rolled it up in a ball and handed it to Margo with thanks. Helena's parents had brought her to the later parade and were now happily taking her home. "Imagine our little girl's picture in the papers!" her father said. Peter looked a little droopy, but his great-grandparents were still chatting away with the mayor.

Margo was feeling tired, too, all of a sudden. She slipped into the car on the front seat next to her mother. Her brother usually hogged the front seat when they went anywhere. But when Margo had said she wanted to go to this parade alone with Mother, Mother had overridden her brother's protest. She'd made him stay home, even though she'd hired a sitter for their little sister, and would not cancel. "Darling, you have done us all proud. You're my true little angel."

Well, so much for Margo's vow to change that image. Mother bent over to kiss her forehead before starting the car, and in the process she knocked the ball of silver lamé and sequins out of Margo's hands. What she said next shocked Margo. It was something about staying out of her bedroom and about how Margo must never help herself to her mother's clothes. Her private things! Her mother had never used such words with her before. Those words did not quite fit a princess image.

CHAPTER SIX

"Winners again!" exclaimed Misty at the next group practice. "That parade was supposed to be a way to celebrate your accomplishments at the school recital. Now we've got to celebrate the celebration!"

All four started talking at once.

"Hold it!" said Misty in that way of hers that no one failed to understand. "We talked celebration plans during practice hour last time only because you had already given a recital that day. I will allow us just three minutes to discuss this. Fall recital is coming up fast. I think it's absolutely necessary that you get in every aspect of training for the bigtime that you can. My discussion first. This celebration *must* be a cast party."

A cast party would surely mean they'd be staying up late again. Margo noticed that Helena had begun a worried prancing even while Misty talked. When there was a pause, Helena said, "Uh-uh, we can't stay up till all hours. My parents are still fussing because I was out past midnight on Halloween." Helena's words were strong though she'd barely whispered them.

Margo said, "My father says I have to live by his rules until I'm old enough to be in charge of my own life. Say, could we have the party before the recital?"

Misty was pleased. "Good thinking. Why not? I know you're going to do well enough at this recital to deserve a celebration, too. If you can handle playing before all those people on Halloween night, then you can handle playing before your parents. We'll celebrate your last two winnings, along with the one you're going to have in two weeks."

"A triple header!" shouted Leroy.

Margo said, "I really did have a good idea. Our parents have to bring us early for pre-performance practice and setup anyway. Then they go back home to pick up the rest of the family. We'll just come ten minutes earlier."

"At the rate you kids eat, that's probably five minutes too long," said Misty. "Big occasions demand creative refreshment tables, so plan wisely what you'll have."

"What will we have?" asked Margo, clapping her head with her hand just to get ideas moving around in there.

"Your three minutes' discussion time is up. All right, play!"

"Brownies and punch," shouted Peter a split-second before his mouth was fastened against his mouthpiece and he was puffing away with the rest.

Margo was afraid Misty would expel him again on the spot, but nothing happened. She could tell, though, that he'd barely escaped it. That fear helped wipe her mind clean of any thought but music. The practice went well.

But once outside, Peter repeated his request that the celebration be brownies and punch.

Margo said, "That's hardly setting a creative table, Peter. I think we should have hors d'oeuvres."

Helena agreed. "The bigtime would have hors d'oeuvres, I guess. We shouldn't eat the same as we eat all the time."

"Well, two votes for *horse's dovers.*" Leroy laughed at his crazy way of saying it, then said, "I know you mean those little crackers with cheese or stuff smeared on them. Hm—only one vote for brownies. I guess that leaves me with the deciding vote." Leroy strutted around a bit before coming back to form a thought huddle.

"Say brownies," whispered Peter, but everyone heard because they were all in the huddle and couldn't help it.

"Hors d'oeuvres," said Leroy.

Peter's chin dropped, but he was a fairly good sport about it. "Our maid makes hors d'oeuvres all the time, even freezes some. We have a freezer full of them. I can bring all you want. The rest of you can bring the punch, so make it root beer. I never get root beer."

"My mother taught me how to make a terrific citrus punch. I'll make that," said Margo.

"I'll bring a pink punch with foam on top," said Helena. "It's my mother's favorite and better than anything Ernestine's mother could make."

"That'll be enough punch," said Leroy. "Just how much punch can four people drink in ten minutes? I'll bring hors d'oeuvres."

"Who'll make them?" Margo asked.

By now they all knew that there was no mother in Leroy's house and that his father cooked. Mostly they had fast food brought in after work. On days when his father had it rough doing his plumbing, he'd just get a huge bag of corn chips out of the cupboard, and he and Leroy would sit and eat them and drink soda pop while watching television. He never asked Leroy to fix dinner, because Leroy had homework to do. After that, Leroy worked on a mathematical cube he was inventing. Each of the six sides would add up to fifteen, no matter if you added a column on the grid going down or across or on the diagonal. And each side would be different. Leroy said it was probably years from being perfected.

"I'll make them myself," declared Leroy.

Everyone groaned, but the matter was closed

since car horns were honking. They had parents to contend with.

Margo kept wishing she had said hors d'oeuvres first instead of letting Peter assign her to punch, but Leroy wouldn't even listen when she called him and proposed a trade. More bad news followed. Helena, of all people, let the word out around school about the preperformance cast party. Then Miss Preston said it would have to include all the students. She wouldn't allow cliques.

When they reported all this to Misty, she was relieved, not mad. "I'm glad Miss Preston will be there," she said. "I have to be in a parade for a late-afternoon football game, and I didn't know how I was going to make it back in time. But I will be there in time for the recital, I can guarantee that."

"But what if something goes wrong?" asked Helena.

Margo had wanted to ask that same question.

Instead she said boldly, "If it does, then we'll use our good minds and cope with it."

"Exactly," said Misty. "Don't make excuses. Winners never bother even thinking up excuses—they think of ways to act. Now you're all winners. Get all those doubts out of your heads. Wipe such junk from your brain cells! Shine like the winners you are!"

Margo's first winning act was to insist to Miss Preston that her original idea remain. It *would* be an hors d'oeuvres and punch party, as her group had planned. When Miss Preston agreed, Margo put her mind to another thing that she knew she could have complete control over: her own clothes.

All participants were to wear white, black, or white *and* black to the recital. However, if someone were forced to go out and buy something new, navy blue would be acceptable. Margo wholeheartedly approved of the reasoning behind this: People should notice the music and not how the performers were dressed.

The only thing was, she knew it never worked. She herself had often sat in the audience when a ballet troupe dressed alike and had spent hours finding the subtle differences. If they all wore different colors, the audience would look for two minutes, their curiosity would be satisfied, and then they would start listening to the recital. Miss Preston hadn't even listened to Margo's suggestion that they wear different colors. It would have been a good excuse for a new dress.

So, Margo went shopping anyway. She didn't tell her parents that she didn't have to buy anything new. Nor did she tell them that they must buy her something new. She simply said, "I'd like to go to the mall to buy a new blouse and skirt for the recital." It worked.

At La Petite Shoppe, to be different, she

bought a white blouse with more ruffles on it than a man's tuxedo shirt. The skirt she chose had pleats near the bottom and on one side. It made her look at *least* eleven. It was navy blue. Then Mother bought her white nylons and navy blue shoes to match the skirt. Mother thought she looked astoundingly stunning—if not positively beautiful—the night of the recital. Well, she'd have to live with that. She had for years.

Dad said the outfit cost more than the music lessons and nothing was tax deductible. But he added, "You look gorgeous, sweetheart," sounding like Humphrey Bogart in one of those old movies he and Mother watched on the VCR. Margo thought she might deliberately smudge her blouse or something.

She dutifully put her citrus punch in a half-gallon Thermos. Then she put the Thermos as well as her mother's fancy glass serving pitcher into a cardboard box for protection, picked up her clarinet case, and was off to the recital quite early.

It turned out that all the mothers had insisted their kids leave early, saying ten minutes was not long enough to carry off a cast party. So everyone was there early, except Leroy. No one waited for him. They ate like wolves. The very, very fancy hors d'oeuvres that Peter had brought were inhaled into empty stomachs on the first go-around. Margo's punch was slurped down so fast it ran like a steady stream until soon she was standing there with an empty pitcher in her hand.

Miss Preston, understandably, was nervous. "Be careful, students. Oh, I'm not at all sure this was such a good idea. I should not have let myself be talked into it. At least I should have insisted it be kept simple."

"My idea was brownies and punch," said Peter.

"Speaking of punch," said Ernestine, who looked ravishingly beautiful in a long black velvet skirt and a blouse identical to Margo's, "I'm afraid that in all the rush I forgot to bring a pitcher. I was hoping there'd be a punch bowl here or something. I can't just pour it from the bottle." She'd brought a bottle of grape juice for punch. Margo couldn't believe it.

"Margo's pitcher is empty. Use that," snapped Miss Preston, and walked away.

"Hold it still for me, Margo, while I pour. Oh dear, oh dear! Accident! Accident! I've gotten it all over your blouse. What will you do? You can't go onstage like that. I guess you'll have to go home."

Margo was steaming. It was one thing for her to want to smudge her own clothes but another to have Ernestine deliberately splash her with grape juice. The juice that hit her navy blue skirt did not show, but on her white blouse it showed dark red instead of purple. She looked as if she had been stabbed. Her parents would be in the audience and would faint dead away to see their daughter wounded. She must spare them.

Margo tried not to cry out for help. She'd told Misty they would cope, and she would. She hissed, "I *am* going on tonight, Ernestine. Later, I'll get you for this and bury you alive. In the meantime, do your family a favor and take out life insurance."

Just then Leroy arrived with a box-lid filled with corn chips with some green stuff piled on each, a little dab on some, big globs on others, and much spilled around the edges.

Margo saw that, but more important she saw that he was wearing a new black suit and a new white shirt. She pushed him over to a corner so fast that he nearly dumped his hors d'oeuvres. "Do you have on an undershirt, Leroy?"

"Of course I have on an undershirt. It's November. What's it to you? What's that on your blouse—blood? You all right, Margo?"

"I am now. Leroy, I want to wear your shirt. Ernestine deliberately spilled grape juice on me. It's not blood. She thought it'd make me run home. We'll show her!"

"Sure we will," said Leroy, already pulling off his suit coat. "My dad won't mind when he hears why."

Margo was more modest than that. She got behind one of the backstage curtains and took off her blouse and then reached out a hand for Leroy's shirt. It didn't look all that bad—sort of like the oversize shirts some of the older girls wore. Leroy buttoned his suitcoat on over his undershirt, and it could have looked worse. It'd give the audience a subtle difference to find during the performance.

About then, the school custodian came over and picked up Margo's blouse where she'd dropped it and handed it to her. "This is a disgusting way for thirteen-year-olds to act."

Well, being taken for thirteen made the night for Margo, who'd have been happy if someone would have given her credit just for being eleven. She felt so good she reached out a finger to clear off a spill from Leroy's box-lid of hors d'oeuvres.

Her tongue was on fire! She'd had just a tiny dab, but her tongue blazed and her eyes watered. "What is that awful hot stuff, Leroy?"

"I don't really know what the proper name for 'em is, but my dad calls them Latin Lovers. We make them with jalapeño peppers. Maybe I'm Latin. I love 'em—eat them all the time."

"We can't serve those, Leroy." Margo said it kindly, but she steeled her eyes for control. She wasn't angry with Leroy. She was delighted with Leroy. "Except to Ernestine," Margo added.

"All right," said Leroy, "I get what you mean."

Margo realized later that she should have left

the offering of the hors d'oeuvres up to Leroy, a boy. Ernestine would never have refused a boy. But she was too impatient, and besides Miss Preston had already called for everyone to find their chairs onstage. "Quick, Ernestine!" Margo whispered. "Try one of Leroy's hors d'oeuvres. He wants you to."

"Why are you so eager, Margo?" Ernestine looked at Margo suspiciously, and then at Leroy standing there. "Are they that good, Leroy?" she asked.

"You bet!" said Leroy. "Here, I'll eat one and show you." He took two of the corn chips with the biggest dollops on them, folded them together like a big bumpy sandwich and started to gulp it.

"Just a minute," said Ernestine, still suspicious. "Let Margo have one first so I can see how good they are."

Margo was on the spot, but she couldn't pull back now. She scanned the box-lid for two chips that Leroy had hardly put any dabs on and quickly grabbed them, put one on top of the other as Leroy had done, and put it into her mouth. She chewed it and swallowed it with a large gulp that seared her vocal cords. She sighed then to allow her voicebox to expel some of the heat and said, "Delicious!"

Then, after exhaling another puff of steam, Margo added, "Those hors d'oeuvres are in a class all their own. I must have the recipe. Are you sure you made them yourself, Leroy?" It was the most control Margo had ever exercised and the best acting she had ever done. She herself was amazed that she could think so well what to say when her mouth and throat and stomach were on fire.

"Sure I made 'em. Here, Ernestine, you can have mine. I'll put another two together for me."

Ernestine took it and raised it to her mouth hesitantly. Leroy was fast in fixing his, so they popped them into their mouths at the same time.

Ernestine bolted for the punch pitcher, which was empty again. Then she shot down the stairs to go for the water fountain out in the hall, but Miss Preston caught her and started pulling her back toward the stage.

By the time Miss Preston had dragged her backstage again, Ernestine was making a grand effort to explain her plight. Miss Preston said, "I'm no good at reading lips. Speak up, girl."

Margo knew Ernestine was too seared to talk. Finally Ernestine did manage to gain her voice and accused Margo of forcing her to burn her insides out.

Miss Preston said, "Margo, is this true?"

"Ask Leroy. He made those particular hors d'oeuvres. I thought they were delicious."

Leroy insisted, "They weren't all that hot.

I've eaten hotter things lots of times." He ate one on the spot to prove how mild they were.

From the look on Miss Preston's face, Margo knew she needed further convincing. And although her own mouth had not cooled at all, she braced herself against the back wall, reached for another shallow filled chip, and ate it. She thought Ernestine was going to crush in on her, looking. But she kept a straight face. Then, as the proof to end all argument, she reached out and took a second one. While they watched solemnly, she ate that, too. She hoped they didn't notice that her jaws had locked and that she'd had to use her finger to pry them open.

Evidently not.

Miss Preston said to Ernestine, "I guess some people just can't take spicy things. Now, hurry to your place."

Margo obeyed. Once in her chair, she let down her forced composure for just a minute and cradled her head in her hands, and moved from side to side in fiery agony. She commanded her musical memory to return, but it would not. She willed memory power to at least flow back into all five of her fingers. Finally she felt it return— one finger at a time. Then, knowing she could carry on, even with her memory a flaming mass of confusion, she straightened up. When the curtain rose, she played her part right on cue.

Ernestine was too shaky to play very well. She did a rotten job on her solo. It got even worse after that.

Margo's performance was passable. Not that playing an entire hour was easy while enduring such suffering. But knowing in her mind that she was avenged enabled her to tolerate her seared tongue quite well. She'd made only a few mistakes—not too bad. Of course, she had done much better during practice times at Misty's. However, Peter and Helena and Leroy played their very best ever. As a group, they'd easily made their thirty percent gain.

She knew she'd still have to reckon with Ernestine in the future, but that was not to be thought of now. She wanted to savor the thrill when Misty dashed backstage and complimented three of her gang royally. Margo herself had not risen to number one. She knew that, but there were two more recitals left before school was out.

CHAPTER SEVEN

Ernestine had gotten the word out around school that Leroy could eat exceedingly hot peppers and never blink an eye. All the sixth-grade boys admired him, and a lot of the girls wrote him notes. Margo thought an awful lot of Leroy, but she just couldn't stand by and let him make such a fool of himself, even if he was having so much fun.

Somebody even brought him a quart of hot peppers and set them on the edge of his desk. He'd eat one every once in a while and bask in the attention. When the teacher ordered him to remove the peppers from the classroom, he simply took them to the music room. Miss Preston couldn't object. She kept a huge gallon jar of dill pickles on the instrument ledge when she was dieting. Miss Preston ate them when hunger pangs hit, and one cost her only ten calories. She said so.

Now, Margo thought those pickles were a real

temptation. Big crunchy garlic dills. But the girls who stuck around the music room weren't after Miss Preston's dills. They were after Leroy. Ernestine was mad for him. So Leroy chased her, caught her, and kissed her. Then other girls would get near him and suddenly start to run so he'd chase them and kiss them, too. It was disgusting the way Leroy enjoyed all that. Margo was about ready to report him herself, but he got caught—by the principal.

He had been chasing Ernestine at the time, and the principal hauled them both toward his office. Leroy looked puzzled and unhappy. As they marched down the hall past Margo, she heard him demand, "What are the rules around here? I didn't know there were any rules in this school against kissing. And I can't even keep hot peppers on my desk!"

"What's all this got to do with hot peppers?" asked the principal.

Ernestine explained. Margo had to trail along to hear how she told it. First Ernestine said, "Margo caused my recital to be ruined by giving me hot pepper hors d'oeuvres! But Leroy's bringing them was not bad. He's innocent enough. He's just an exceptional boy who can eat a hot pepper and never blink an eye. But Margo did what she did deliberately. Don't worry. My mother plans to come see you about it."

The principal caught Margo listening and

grabbed her by the arm. "You come into the office, too, young lady. A pretty little thing like you, acting like that. I'm surprised."

The principal phoned Ernestine's mother to save her the trip. He had to move the receiver out away from his ear. Even Margo could hear the angry blast being shouted through it. Ernestine's mother was threatening to sue the school and Margo's parents.

Next, the principal called Margo's mother. Mother said she'd call Father. Margo found out later that Father called Ernestine's mother back with, "Hello, this is Attorney Girard calling. Did you have a complaint about my daughter Margo?"

That sort of ended the whole run-around. And for some reason it ended things between Ernestine and Leroy as well. It seemed that Leroy's father had done some plumbing for Ernestine's mother that she'd found unsatisfactory. No one could ever please that woman.

Anyway, Margo learned that all things work out if they are allowed to run their course. Leroy stopped chasing and kissing girls. He and Margo became good friends again. But not before Leroy had reported it to Peter, and Margo had reported it to Helena, and either Peter or Helena had reported it to Misty.

Misty said what they all needed was some fresh air and exercise and that the next group rehearsal would be held on the football field.

"Please notify your parents. One of these days you'll all be part of a marching band, no doubt, and you might as well have some advance practice marching during halftime. It'll be good for you."

No one objected. In fact, they were all happy to get consent from their parents. Father gave his begrudgingly.

"Does Misty charge extra for these fresh-air practices?" Father grumbled. "The next thing, she'll be wanting to outfit you all in band uniforms. Maybe it's time to yell, 'Stop the music!'" Then he looked at Margo, who from habit had pulled a sweet, sad face. He said, "Get into the car, Muffy. If I'm taking you to the football field, it's time we got started."

Still, Father questioned Misty when they got there. "What do you have in mind to do?"

"Nothing big today," answered Misty pleasantly. "Just marching in the wind around the football field. Musicians do not always have to be cooped up indoors like captured beasts. They deserve the right to open-air performances. What if your son's soccer team had to practice only in your garage?" Misty laughed.

That was hardly feasible, but Father was the soccer coach and Misty had made her point. Father said to Margo, "Use the hood on your windbreaker," and zoomed away.

Helena's mother said to Misty, "I want you to take right good care of my little girl out there on that big football field. You'll have your hands full minding all them kids."

"We'll manage," Misty assured her.

Peter's great-grandparents thought it was a grand idea. They had donated that football field to the community.

Leroy's father just dumped him off and buzzed away to finish a plumbing job before he had to be back for pick-up.

To the rasping beat of Leroy's snare drum, the five began to march around the football field. Misty led the way, wearing her kilts and high-stepping it in her leather boots for the first few feet. Then she did an in-place bit of high-stepping until Peter came alongside so she could help him manage his tuba. Then all went wonderfully well.

Margo was almost certain she heard thunderous applause as they swept out into the center of the field and snaked around it from side to side. But after thirty minutes of marching and trying to remember notes and whether to puff and blow or toot or rasp, everyone declared exhaustion. At Margo's suggestion, they dashed for the bleachers and collapsed.

Within seconds Leroy was no longer content to sit on the first row to rest, so he scampered like a monkey to higher bleachers.

"Let's all go!" sang Margo, waving her clarinet as she climbed. Helena was right behind her. Peter laid his tuba down first and then climbed up to them. At that cue they all put down their instruments at whatever bleacher they had reached so they could climb more freely.

Leroy was only one step ahead of Margo, and his toe touched her clarinet. It toppled over, bell end first, into the space between the bleacher seat and the footrest. Margo slid in a way that would make any baseball player jealous and grabbed it just in time. Unfortunately, this particular place was near two closely spaced supporting beams. Her beloved clarinet had managed to slip in but the clarinet and her clenched fist would not come out. If she unclenched her fist, the clarinet would drop all the way down to the ground behind and, at the very least, be dented.

"Try reaching your other hand in and around to the back of the beam to hold on," Leroy suggested. His voice sounded sort of pleading. He must feel terrible about being the cause.

"Hold on to what—thin air? My arm's not that long. I can't reach to the back of the beam."

Neither could Leroy nor Misty. Those two had the longest arms, so neither Peter or Helena tried.

Margo wailed, "I don't think my clarinet will survive this. And I won't survive if I force my hand out. I'll lose an inch of skin and bone."

"You'll survive," said Misty. *"How* has not been determined yet, but you and your clarinet will survive."

"I was bitten by a rabid dog once, and I survived. And I was only three," said Helena.

"I lost my hearing in one of my ears, so I'm not much good on the guitar or fiddle like my dad, but I survived. I play the drums," said Leroy.

"I'm the only kid in four generations, and my great-grandparents can't hear half of what I say. If I had an emergency on the maid's day off, I'd be in for it. But—"

"Cut it out!" cried Margo. She really was crying. The wind was tangling her blond hair across her wet cheeks until she could hardly see all these noble survivors standing around her. She had not pulled up the hood on her windbreaker. Now she wished she had. Now she wished she had laid her clarinet down on the bottom step before she had climbed the bleachers. Her hand was becoming exhausted from the reach and the grasp. She didn't know how much longer she could hold out.

"We better call the police," said Helena.

"You know very well by the time it'd take even Leroy with his long legs to deliver a message to the police, they'd never make it back to this football field before my fingers let go."

"We'll all get underneath and catch it when you let it fall," suggested Peter. They all ran away to do that, leaving Margo alone. But in a minute they were back, saying that the end of the bleachers was boxed in.

"Must be to keep kids from hiding under there during football games. There was a little plank door at the end of each set of bleachers—no doubt for a clean-up after games—but it was padlocked," explained Leroy.

Margo willed herself to come up with a really super idea for the survival of her clarinet, but it didn't happen. She suggested that maybe the padlock was rusty and could be broken open with a little force, but Leroy assured her that it was highly polished and new.

"Well, couldn't you find the remains of a greasy hamburger from last night's game and grease my hand so it would slip out easily and not get hurt?" No one answered that. So much for dreaming. She knew none of those silly wishes would come true.

She dropped it, finally, with a great howl of woe. Her beautiful clarinet slipped from her exhausted fist. She had lost her chance at happiness. She thought she would die. Father was still making installment payments on it. It certainly didn't look as if this experience was going to work itself out right this time.

They were all standing there in silence watching while Margo massaged her hand when Leroy's father appeared. He had gotten his job over with quickly, and having once played on this very football field, he strolled in early—for old time's sake, he said. Leroy wasn't listening. He ran to his dad's truck and returned with a crowbar. He had a board off the end of the bleachers in no time. He let Margo be the first one through the hole. The others followed to help find the clarinet and survey the damage.

The clarinet had a dent and a scratch—nothing that couldn't be fixed. Margo was glad it was no worse, but she felt a year's allowance slip away. Father would think she was irresponsible.

"Look what else I found!" shouted Peter, who'd been rummaging around in the garbage. He probably had never been in such an unclean place before. He held up a twenty-dollar bill.

The hunt was on. Right away Margo found a nickel and two dimes. The others found some quarters, one half dollar, and loads of pennies. No more bills were found, not even a single dollar bill. Still, the total came to twenty-nine dollars and six cents.

"No wonder they padlock under the bleachers!" said Margo. "Wow! All that money lost when excited fans reach into their pockets or purses to get change for treats." Margo felt like volunteering to the city to clean up at the end of the season.

Leroy's father nailed the board back into place, and they were all heading toward the gate by the time practice usually ended. The other three cars had pulled in and were waiting. Peter was lagging behind with his tuba and called out, "Wait! Wait!"

Margo thought he just wanted help carrying it, so she didn't slow down. They weren't marching now, just going home. Misty had told her and everyone at the beginning that Peter was responsible for his instrument the same as they were responsible for the instrument of their choice. Each instrument had assets and drawbacks. Peter must learn to live with the tuba's size. But Peter's continued call made Margo finally stop.

He caught up with her and huffed out the words. "Here, Margo, is the twenty dollars. You'll need it to get the dent pinged out. I'd never have found it if you hadn't lost your clarinet through that crack. I know how I'd have felt if it'd been my tuba."

"It couldn't have been your tuba," declared Leroy. "A crack big enough for it to fall through would have been called a door, and we could all have jumped through it to help." Leroy reached into his jeans pocket and brought out a handful of change and dropped it into Margo's pocket. "Take this, too. It was my toe that tipped your clarinet."

Margo couldn't say a word.

Then Helena, Misty, and Leroy's dad gave

up their found money, too. "What are friends for?" they said when Margo protested.

So, Margo was crying again and the wind was matting and tangling her hair against her wet cheeks as she went toward her waiting father. But she was smiling.

"Didn't I tell you to pull the hood up on your head?" her father called. As she got into the car, he noticed she was exceptionally dirty and asked, "Where've you been? You've been crying! What's the matter, Muffy? Did you get hurt? Why are you smiling like that?"

Margo dumped all the money onto the car seat beside her father and told him the entire story. What could he do but say, "Well, I'll be darned! Funny how things can work themselves out like that. Some friends you got there."

"Yeah," said Margo, and with her clarinet safely seat-belted onto her lap, she leaned her head back on the soft headrest and fell asleep.

CHAPTER EIGHT

I hope you can stand the smell of candy cooking while I listen," said Misty.

The smell didn't distract Margo nearly as much as the watching. That was almost irresistible. Christmas was definitely in the air, what with all the talk of gift getting and gift giving. Misty was making candy to give away. She was testing it now for doneness. A frail thread stretched thinner and thinner as she held the testing spoon high in the air.

Reluctantly, Margo looked back at her sheet music. Then the smell really hit her. She tried to think music, music, music. Misty had said, "Isolate your mind from all but your music, and you can practice anywhere. It's very important that you learn not to be distracted by things around you."

Uhm—Margo tried. *Think sheet music full of notes. Read those notes and play them.* How did kids practice in the olden days before written music was invented? She played the first line. Then the second. And the third. Misty gave her usual approval and advice, and somehow Margo managed to finish the hour.

"Pretty good," said Misty. "All you kids are doing very well. I think after that march around the football field, you four will be ready to do a project on your own. Keep that in mind, will you? In the meantime, I've got one more scheme for you. I'll discuss it when all of you are here next Friday. Time's up."

"You're mean," said Margo as she gently packed her repaired clarinet.

Misty laughed and pushed her toward the door and out into the cold December air away from the smells of Christmas cooking. Mother never made Christmas candy; she bought it at the mall. Margo was going to make her own when she grew up.

After Margo had switched practice days with Peter, her day was Tuesday. That meant she'd have three whole days before she could find out what the new plans were.

On Friday, Misty handed them some new sheet music for two Christmas songs that Miss Preston had already had them learn at school. "I wanted you to have your own sheet music. You'll need to look professional and orderly. You're going to perform at the mall on December twenty-first at four o'clock."

"At the mall!" No one could believe it.

"I contacted the mall manager and set the date today. You've played before your classmates, you've played before your parents, you've played in a parade, and you've practiced to play for halftime at a football game. Now you're ready to rehearse before hundreds of people. This is a very strategic thing to do. You must get used to the crowds so that when you're in grand auditoriums, you'll be calm and your minds will be only on your music. Nothing must distract you then. It won't if you've rehearsed before many people a few times."

Margo knew Misty spoke the truth. But it would be a sad practice. It would be Peter's last time to play with them before he had to leave. Margo tried to think of some way to give him a grand send-off. She didn't want him to go home after Christmas. She thought about it while seriously practicing and appreciating the songs she'd taken for granted only the day before. Then she proudly took her new sheet music home to show her parents.

Mother was more impressed with this Christmas adventure than by any of their other adventures. She got out her very finest stationery and said, "All our friends and relatives who live nearby will be coming to the mall to Christmas shop. I'm going to send them each a note to be sure to be there on the twenty-first to see our Muffy."

Father said, "How about that? Here, let me see what you'll be playing, Muffy. Oh, 'Rudolph' and 'Jingle Bells.' Peppy tunes, those. You'll do great, sweetheart."

Even her older brother leaned over Father's shoulder, and her younger sister piled all over Father's lap to look at the sheet music and neither of them could read music. Only Margo could do that. Not well, but she was learning fast. She was happy about all the excitement this created in the family. She would do her best and make them really proud. She'd be number one.

"Oops! Careful with Margo's sheet music!" said Father.

Her little sister had crumpled it while horsing around on Father's lap, trying to keep their brother from getting a close look.

"Aw, Father, you've let them ruin it! What will Misty say when she sees this?" What Margo wanted to do was roll up the pitiful-looking sheet and swat everyone a good one. But Misty would not have approved of that action. She could have told Margo, "They are happy for you. They will be your audience. Do you want to hit them? Find another way to cope. Winners are known for finding better ways to cope. Margo, you're a winner."

So she ironed it.

It didn't look too bad when she took it again for practice, nor when she took it to the mall on the twenty-first at three-thirty. Her mother and brother and sister came along. Margo parted with them as soon as she spotted Leroy and Helena, who were checking the mall guide for the performers' waiting room.

The three of them walked along together among the bustling crowd until they got near Foley's, where there was an after-school special. Foley's doors had been closed for thirty minutes to let the shoppers who were already there finish. For the next two hours only they would be offering a twenty percent discount and free wrapping to any kid under sixteen who bought a gift for his or her parents.

The place was teeming with children and their parents waiting for the doors to open again. They blocked the entire walkway. Margo and her friends had to worm their way through if they hoped to give a musical performance on the other side.

Margo said, "Obstacles will always arise. You can count on it. Never let it stop us. Charge!" She was beginning to sound like Misty. She pushed her way through. Leroy followed, then Helena. But the mad, stirring crowd thought they were trying to push in front and fought them back.

Margo got through to Misty, who was on the wooden platform provided for performers. Leroy finally made it, too. But Helena did not come out on the other side at all.

Misty reached out a hand to pull them up

the stairs. Margo shook her head. "I can't. I'm going back to help Helena."

"We can see over the crowd from up here," Misty explained, pulling her up onto the platform. That was true. Margo spotted Helena about halfway through, in front of a mannequin whose clothes were changed each day. It stood in the middle of the walkway.

"I see her. I'd better go get Helena," Margo insisted.

"I'll do it," offered Leroy.

Did Misty give them permission to go? Or offer to go herself? Indeed not. She just stood there restraining them on the platform while she *shouted* encouragement to Helena. The program announcer stood to one side unsmiling, listening. A little crowd of Margo's mother's friends and some relatives had already gathered. They stood waiting for Margo to perform. She didn't want to let them down, but Helena was her friend and needed help. "People have been trampled to death in crowds," she explained to Misty.

"We've got to trust Helena to make it. It's four o'clock. Where's Peter?" said Misty.

Oh, no, was Misty thinking of expelling him again for tardiness at a time like this? And what about Helena? With relatives watching her every move, Margo hesitated to shout to Helena. Mother would be embarrassed. But Margo wanted to with a passion. She tried willing Helena to hurry by using mental telepathy. She'd read all about such things, and this was the time to try it out.

Misty called again to Helena, but she stopped and said abruptly to Margo, "Are you chewing gum?" At a time like this Misty *would* ask a question like that!

Margo was chewing gum—and rather rapidly, too. She took it out, expecting to be expelled right then and there. In front of her entire family she would get the ax. Then she saw the huge clock on the mall wall. One minute until four. "Not practice time yet," she told Misty with no defiance but with great joy at being saved.

"My watch says it's four," Misty retorted, and called once more to Helena.

"But we're practicing in the mall. We have to go by mall time. You can't expel me! Are you going to expel Helena and Peter?"

"I'm worried about Peter" was all that Misty said.

Suddenly there was Helena, standing with her flute, on the raised base of the mannequin, the place where a woman usually stood to dress it daily. She waved her flute case.

Next, they saw Peter. Actually, it was the tip of his tuba that they saw. Peter had once told Margo that he loved that tuba because it made him feel big and as if he were not the only child in four generations of adults. Margo was thankful for its bigness now, for it let them spot Peter and know that he was alive. Even Misty looked relieved. Maybe she would not expel those two kids who were caught in the teeming masses.

Suddenly Peter was blotted out by the crowd. Then the tuba appeared again, slightly to the left, not far from Helena. Then the tip of it began to rise; then Peter's head, shoulders . . . then there he was squeezed onto the platform next to Helena, talking to her. Then, as Helena steadied him, he lifted the mouthpiece to his mouth and gave a blast. Talk about projection! The whole crowd turned. At which point Peter called out, "Let us through, and we'll get onto the stage and play for you."

Now Margo knew her good friends would not be expelled. There was nothing in this world Misty liked better than to know they'd coped with a situation. Helena and Peter had coped beautifully. The crowd parted. The four were once again together, side by side, with instruments ready. Misty clapped her hands like cymbals, and they began "Jingle Bells."

The crowd in front of Foley's began to sing along, clapping occasionally for emphasis. They sang "Rudolph the Red-Nosed Reindeer" as well and yelled for more. So the four did encores until Foley's opened the doors for their after-school special.

Margo's family and friends crowded the stage to congratulate her, saying she was the best player in the world. But she saw her friends were getting the same treatment and hearing the same praise. Oh, well, she guessed they were all number ones. When at last her mother and the others announced it was time to shop, Misty explained to the parents that it was customary for them to celebrate every success. This had been a grand one. So she asked for and got permission to take the four for a treat. Margo was very pleased and flattered, even though she knew this must be in Peter's honor.

Misty took them into Weber's for red raspberry and green mint malts—specials for the Christmas crowd. "Well, gang, I'm proud of you all. You're real troopers. Have been all along. Leroy brought his Dad's crowbar when he needed to get underneath the football bleachers. Margo had the courage to borrow Leroy's shirt when her blouse was ruined. Helena lost her shyness today and came out in high places. Peter . . ." Here Misty paused. "Peter gave a grand blast as his swan song. Oh, Peter, we sure hate to lose you!"

Margo wished she had said all that.

"I don't want to leave," said Peter sorrowfully. "But one more day of school is all I've got here, and then I'm off to live in Boston. My mother and father got back from their around-the-world trip, you know. They were standing out there today with my great-grandparents. So were my grandparents. They all say I'm a chip off the old block, the way I handled that crowd. They think this is going to be a happy holiday with all of us together." Peter's voice became even more downcast. He slurped the bottom of his malt with a rasping noise.

"Good!" sang Margo. "We have them all together, so we can talk to them and make them let you stay until school's out and we can have our end-of-the-year recital together."

Instant agreement came from all but Misty. Then Misty shook her head and said, "Oh, what the heck. Go ahead and try, Margo. I've always known you kids were going to make it in music. And now I'm beginning to believe you can do anything."

CHAPTER NINE

She failed. She failed miserably. At first Margo felt that luck was really riding with them to have all six—Peter's parents, grandparents, and great-grandparents—there at the mall performance. She confronted them all, insisting that Peter had to stay. The answers she'd gotten were "nos," "indeed nots," and "emphatically nots."

How Peter ever survived such strong adult forces was a miracle. But then at other times they spoiled him. It all equals out in the world, Margo guessed. That gave her an idea. She whispered to Peter, and he in turn did a superb job of carrying out her suggestion.

"Take back any Christmas presents you've purchased for me! Just let me stay here for the spring recital at school and the big June recital. It's all I'll ever ask for in my entire life."

Such eloquence! Margo stood in awe.

Peter's father said, "You hardly know what you're saying. You're too young to know what you'll want the rest of your life."

His mother said, "Your presents have been lovingly and thoughtfully purchased all over the world. We can hardly return them. You'll accept them graciously and enjoy this Christmas as you always have. We'll hear no more from any of you." She looked sharply at Margo.

So Margo and the other three went to their homes very sadly. It was only four days until Christmas. To be sad four days before Christmas was un-American.

At school the next day, Margo, Leroy, and Helena put their heads together in a huddle like football players do when they have big and important decisions to make. "Whatever we decide will affect whether or not Peter stays. We had better decide well," counseled Margo.

Ernestine tried to listen. She was wild to know all secrets. "You're giving a special gift to Miss Preston—that's what you're planning."

"No, Ernestine. Go away. This is far more serious than that," said Margo.

"You're going to do something rotten to somebody?"

"No," said Helena.

"And that somebody's me! I knew it! Planning horrible things like that, and it's the last day of school before Christmas. I'm going to report you all."

"No! Get out of here, Ernestine, or I'll *sack* you," said Leroy.

"You're going to tell about the special setup I'm using on my tomato plants for the science fair so others can do the same thing!" Leroy's dad had gone back to fix the plumbing job he'd done at Ernestine's so they did know of her experiment. Gravel from her experiment had clogged the pipes.

"Thanks, Ernestine. You've solved our problem," said Margo.

"What problem? What have I solved?"

"Peter has to be in the science fair. Our school system puts more emphasis on science than any—well, just anywhere!" sang Margo.

"Yeah. Best in the nation," agreed Leroy. "Even the private schools get in on it. The Bentons would never deny Peter the best in education. Already they have enrolled him at Stanford for college. I think that's what Peter said."

It worked, thanks to Ernestine's stupid suggestion and jealousy. Reluctantly, Peter's parents stayed on for two weeks with him. His father admitted they did have some business they had cut short, and since it meant so very much to Peter . . . and since they had never seen him happier . . . They drove him to group practice, kissed him a weeping good-bye, and told him to make them proud with his science experiment. Then they shook hands with the gang and left Peter for the rest of the school year to his wonderful great-grandparents. And to Misty. And to his very best friends in all the world.

"Well, that's settled," said Margo. "Now on to our next big problem: What can Peter do that's extraordinary at the science fair?"

"You could run a test on different shampoos," said Helena. "Only I've already started that." She'd been saving the little sample bottles for two years. "I could share."

Leroy said he was doing subsoil samples. He said his father often had to dig to replace sump pumps or, on occasion, to replace a well out in the country, and he got to see how soil changes as you dig down deep into it. He'd draw a graph with the water-seepage scale carefully calculated. Peter said to count him out on both.

Margo's superplan was to ask her grandfather, who worked with industrial diamonds, if he would help her do a test for comparative hardness. Nobody, even the high school kids, would have a chance like that. But her father had said, "It's sort of silly to do that in sixth grade. What could you do for an encore?"

Peter's family was knowledgeable about the stock market, but they had no ideas for him for a science experiment. Peter was really down in the dumps. He phoned Margo and said, "Come over here, and we'll discuss it. I know some really good ideas will come out if you talk long enough. Besides, you could watch my snakes with me."

Margo could hardly resist such flattery, but the last statement made her say, "We'll just talk on the phone, Peter, if you don't mind. To be perfectly honest, Peter, I hate snakes. I always have."

"That's a stupid reason, Margo."

"They are slick and slimy, and they bite and look mean and jump out at you when you least expect it. Sorry, Peter. I like you, but I don't like your snakes. I just never told you that before because you never pressed me before." Peter had been gasping and fuming and sputtering until she could hardly finish her words.

"You are the most misinformed person about snakes in all the world!"

Peter shouted so loud Margo could hear his great-grandmother in the background saying, "Now, now, Peter. Remember your telephone manners"—and she was hard of hearing.

"I won't come, Peter, and that's final."

"Okay, no snake watching. Just come over, please."

"I'll ask Father if he'll take me. Hold on."

Father was very happy to get a few more minutes in the mansion and a chance to discuss taxes with the Bentons. He made Margo be a good sport and go look at Peter's snakes. He wanted more time with the Bentons.

First, Peter explained, "Snakes are not slick or slimy. Just touch this one, Margo, and you'll see."

Margo said, "I didn't come here to touch a snake."

Her father, who stood on the other side of their cage, said, "Nothing to it, Margo. Just reach a finger in and touch toward his tail. Watch me."

"Don't touch that one! He's feeling sort of low today. I never disturb them when they're not feeling well."

"Um, well, sorry about that, Peter. Anything we can do to help?"

"Nothing. Most animals just want to rest until nature heals them. I just don't want him disturbed, that's all."

Margo could tell that her father was feeling awkward for having done something wrong. She felt that way herself at times. So she helped by saying, "At least you and I can rehearse together while Father walks around. I have my clarinet in the car."

"Okay," said Peter. "I'll get my tuba."

Because the clarinet was much smaller and Margo was an ace runner, she got back before Peter. He was not an ace runner and had to go up to the second floor. She got out her clarinet and began warming up.

At last, when Peter came bumping in with his tuba, he just set it down and gawked. Finally Margo turned to see what held him so fascinated. "Look who's moving!" sang Peter, paying no attention to his tuba.

Margo looked, but she didn't see any of them moving.

"Play your clarinet again."

She played, and the snake that had been feeling low began to move. "You're a snake charmer, Margo!" Peter shouted.

"I don't want to be a snake charmer."

"Well, you are, like it or not. See—when you stopped, it stopped! Play again."

She played, and Peter rested his case. Then he said, "Just a minute—let me try the tuba." It took him a minute to set up, but the snake did not respond to his notes. He was more than a little hurt by that.

"Margo, I think we've got my science experiment. I'll record how music excites or calms snakes. You'll have to be my partner—I don't play the clarinet."

"I might, and I might not," said Margo. She hesitated to tell Peter or anyone that she'd called her grandfather that very afternoon and that he'd refused to help her on the diamond experiment. He'd said, "Muffy, we'll do that one when you get into high school. Why don't you do something on how long eleven-year-olds can hold their breath, or whatever." Imagine such rejection and such a silly suggestion! But here Peter was just begging to work with her. It helped her recover from the rejection.

She did a bit more playing, and Peter kept a record of all the snakes' activity and dated his ledger as any good scientist would. Pretty soon

Father and Peter's great-grandmother came in. Father told Margo it was time to leave. Peter's great-grandmother asked why only Margo was practicing and why Peter was letting his tuba sit idle.

Peter explained all that had happened and ended by saying, "Margo could make a lot of money going into the snake-charming business. People in India do it all the time. They make millions."

"Well, hardly millions," said his great-grandmother. "But that is a wonderful idea you two have come up with and that was very good playing for a thirteen-year-old girl."

While Margo beamed at that age mistake, Peter and Father were quick with the correction. Peter said, "She's eleven—my age exactly." It didn't take any of the joy away, though. It was the second time someone had made that mistake, so it meant that people were seeing her as an older girl. That's all that mattered.

"I'll do it, Peter. I'll be your partner."

Father was very pleased that his daughter was entering a project in the science fair with the Benton boy. He whistled all the way home. Mother wasn't quite so thrilled when she found out what the project was.

What was really nice was that Leroy and Helena both decided to get into the act as well. While Helena was at school, her mother had been using all the shampoo from Helena's little sample bottles. "She thought I was just saving bottles and didn't want the shampoo to go to waste. So I'll play music for snakes, and I'll tell her so!" Helena said with her new boldness.

Leroy's father said he'd had no sump pumps or wells to repair for months and might not have one before summer. He could guarantee Leroy nothing except that he didn't plan to go out and damage one for the sake of a silly science experiment. "So," said Leroy, "my calculations will be on the number of different reactions the snakes have to music. They're here and waiting. Misty will love it! This is our very own idea, and she's had nothing to do with it. Shall we tell her?"

"No. Let's win the prize first and then tell her."

"We won't tell anyone! We'll surprise the whole science fair!"

So it was set. "Secrecy and hard work" was their motto.

The good news from school was that all Ernestine's tomatoes died when her family went away for the weekend and their cat pulled on the edge of the tray and dumped the plants, gravel, water, and vitamins onto the carpet.

The bad news from school was that Ernestine had overheard Margo telling about her grandfather's silly suggestion about breath-holding for a project and thought it was neat. She had taken a friend as a partner, and they were getting all kinds of attention.

Her friend's father was an obstetrician. So they got from him a long-nosed micrometer, which looked sort of like ice tongs. The doctor used that instrument to measure the diameter of babies' heads. The girls used it to measure the distance between their sucked-in stomachs and their backbones. Some kids can just naturally suck in their stomachs farther than others when they hold their breath. Everyone cooperated with them. To Ernestine's delight, Leroy held the record. She took readings on full stomachs as well as empty ones. No one knew what she was trying to prove by it. When Margo asked Ernestine, she had a ready answer.

"This is a *pure* science experiment. A fact is a fact, whether it's to be put to use now or years from now."

That made so much sense it made Margo furious. Even worse, Ernestine got written up in the local newspaper. After that, kids came running to her as quickly as they would run to a filled cookie jar. In the end, because Margo was the only one in class who had not cooperated, she, too, had to allow her sucked-in stomach to be measured.

With all her might she sucked in her breath and held it and held it. Ernestine was being clumsy and slow. Margo knew she was waiting for her to exhale and then she'd record some big number. She didn't care if she passed out. She would not exhale until this was done properly. Leroy finally grabbed the micrometer and said the reading aloud. Margo was able to exhale and live.

But she thought she'd die if Ernestine won first prize for the few sixth graders represented at the fair. It was such a grand idea, and everyone was betting on her to win—just everybody! It made Margo want to reveal her gang's superproject. But she had taken an oath never to reveal it until Peter's snakes were at the fair, and then would come the moment of unveiling and their triumph. They would win.

It's very hard to live with any secrets locked in your head. It took a lot of mastery to hold secret such a mystery. Why, they even had Misty mystified! She kept saying how much their musical talents were being honed and polished and that they must be really putting in practice time on their days off. But she didn't understand why they played some pieces now in low crooning notes, pieces they used to blast out.

Margo made the mistake of telling Ernestine and others that she was going to be in the science fair but that her project was a secret. Ernestine was no fool. She was a rival to be reckoned with. She said, "If you are planning to do the same thing to me that you did at the Halloween parade and include music, forget it. Music is barred from this science fair."

Margo reported that to her friends, of course. Leroy said, "That may be so, and then again it may not. Ernestine has a doctor's degree in lying."

"If she's lying, I'll bury her alive. No—I'll snatch her up and throw her into a tank of live and very hungry piranhas," said Margo.

"I'm going to go ask the principal," said Helena and did so. She reported back two minutes later. "This is not a music fair, so there is to be none unless you are studying the science of music or something like that. We've got nothing to worry about."

"Ha!" said Margo. "Ernestine has a Ph.D., a J.D., an M.D., an M.B.A., and an I.E. in lying!" She used all the initials she'd ever heard her father mention. "She'll give us even more trouble on the day of the fair, when she sees us with our instruments. You can bet on it. So let's be prepared."

Margo was exactly right. On the day of the fair, when they marched in with the snakes in a crate and instruments in hand, Ernestine was waiting. She was wearing a badge with her name, her project's title, and her booth number on it. All she'd had to bring was a graph of her statistics about how many inches there were from a kid's sucked-in stomach to backbone. Big deal.

"Music is barred. I checked it out. No entertainment allowed. We can decorate the booths all we wish, but no music. I told you so. Too bad, Margo."

With great control Margo did not answer but marched right by Ernestine, holding the handle of her clarinet case tightly in one hand and Peter's tuba in the other. Helena carried her violin case and Leroy's drums. Leroy helped Peter carry the crate of snakes. It was covered with a sheet. They were all anxiously awaiting the time of the unveiling. Wouldn't the crowd go wild with surprise? All they needed now was to find out where their booth was to be set up.

None of them was prepared for the answer the woman at the long table of spread-out badges gave them. "I'm sorry, your name doesn't seem to be here. Are you sure you registered?"

"Of course we didn't!" said Leroy. "We didn't plan to register until we got here. Our project is a surprise."

"I'm afraid that's not quite how it's done. We aren't prepared for surprises here. It's enough for us to keep ahead of things when we know what *is* coming. Didn't you get your entry forms?"

All four pulled their filled-in forms from their pockets and handed them to her.

"Not to me. No, no, my dears. No. I couldn't handle all that at the last minute. This was to be turned in to your school leaders. If there's an extra booth, perhaps you can set up and have the experience, since you're already here. But I'm afraid you're barred from competition."

Margo was furious and hurt. From the looks of her friends, she knew they were, too. She tried to remember if it was her idea or whose. Had she been the one to suggest they not enter until the last possible moment to keep their surprise a grand secret?

"Snakes need a lot of care and attention," said Peter, "and I've given mine the best. But our project's not about their care. It's—"

"Snakes? You have snakes in that crate?"

"Well, yes, ma'am. Ten." Peter lifted the sheet.

The woman's scream and fast departure got them the attention they had all hoped for. People came crowding in. Leroy kept them held back on one side, and Margo on the other. While Peter set the crate on top of the badge table, Helena began playing her flute, and the snakes began to move. Fascination kept the crowd quiet for a moment. So Margo was able to take out her precious instrument, and she began to play as well. Black, beady eyes in flat heads swayed as bodies coiled and recoiled.

Ernestine was right there in front; her green eyes bugged out as if someone had seized her by the throat. "Ugly!" she said. "They're . . ." She was lost to find a suitably disgusting word and substituted an ugly facial expression instead.

"They're very interesting creatures," supplied Leroy. He unrolled a chart as if it were an ancient scroll and presented it left and right, fore and aft, for all to view. "Here are but a few statistics. At the top you'll see the headings: Snakes at rest. Snakes' movements when food arrives. Snakes' movements when provoked. Snakes' movements when loud music is played. Snakes' movements when soft music is played."

"All right! All right, back to your booths. This is a science fair, not a circus. You kids there—if you're not registered, I'll have to ask you to take your snakes and go home," said the principal in charge of the fair.

"We tried to register, but we weren't allowed to do it. Here are the forms to prove it." Margo handed over their forms. Peter covered the snakes, and Helena put her flute back into its case. Leroy walked away for some reason Margo didn't know. It seemed like a poor time to leave the three of them holding the bag—or crate.

By the time the principal finished arguing with Margo, then with Peter, and, for a surprisingly long time with Helena, Leroy had returned with Misty. He'd called, and Misty had come!

They hugged her and informed her and beseeched her to act in their behalf with this uncaring person.

She hugged them back, took careful note of all the information they supplied, and refused them outright. "Hold it. I accept all your words as the truth. You've always been an honest lot from the start. Lousy musicians at first, but honest kids. Your musical ability has vastly improved, and you've lost none of your honesty in the process, and for this I'm very pleased. You're also not officially registered for this science fair, and out the door you go. Let's move it."

Margo almost dropped her clarinet at such disappointment. If she dented it again, her father would never forgive her, and she wouldn't be able to get it repaired in time for the next recital, where she was going to outplay Ernestine like she'd never been outplayed in her life. Margo realized the danger her precious horn was in and tightened her hand around it. She gently placed it into its cushioned box.

Once the troupe got their gear outside the building, Misty stopped them and asked, "If you want to say something to me, say it now. Don't let it mushroom out of proportion."

"I'd like to say a lot of things. I have a list a mile long. I guess I'll shorten it to: you were supposed to *help* us!" said Margo.

"Oh, I am helping you. I am," said Misty. "Why don't you boys put that crate down right over there? Um . . . let's see, you musicians could stand right over there. Street musicians, if they're smart, try to catch the crowds coming and going."

Not one word more was needed from Misty.

They all became instant street musicians with a snake-charming show that out-Indiaed India. Those four were no dummies. And they caught the crowds coming and going. Parents couldn't get enough of taking their pictures or taking pictures with their own kids squatting beside the snakes. It was terrific.

Ernestine and her friends came marching out at the tail end of the day carrying some sort of ribbon or other. It made no difference to Margo. She and her friends were too busy counting their own bounty for the day. Leroy had conveniently placed his plumber's cap near the corner of the snake crate, and all those picture-taking parents had obligingly tossed in quarters and even dollars. Being the sixth-grade math whiz that he was, Leroy had divided it equally among them within seconds of the final counting. $16.75 each.

Peter used a dollar of his money to buy back a Polaroid shot of his snake exhibit, the magnificent scroll of statistics, and the musicians. He was certain it would make his parents very happy. They'd display that picture in a prominent place on the mantel for years and explain to guests the sacrifice they'd suffered from being away from Peter for so very long, but hadn't it been worth it?

They decided not to tell their parents about the money they had earned. Father had convinced all the gang's parents to invest the money earned from the Halloween parade in bonds. But they wanted to spend this money and would when the right thing came along.

Margo's father came at the same time Peter's great-grandfather arrived. The two of them had become good friends. He helped Mr. Benton load the snake crate into the trunk of the Cadillac. Then he lifted Margo up and swung her around a couple of times, the way he used to do when she was very small, and plopped her into the backseat of their car. "You have a good day dabbling in science, Muffy?"

"A perfect day," said Margo. "Only . . ."

"Yeah?"

"Only Misty helped us. At the next recital we're going to do it totally by ourselves. Totally!"

"You betcha, sweetheart," Father said with a nasal twang that made Margo crack up. Maybe it wasn't all that funny, but then again maybe it was. Anyway, she and her father sure thought it was.

CHAPTER TEN

*E*veryone knew that the really big recital, the acid test, was the one at the end of the school year. Would the gang's musical skills match Ernestine's at the next recital and rise a notch higher still at the final one?

Each and every practice was very serious business. Misty told them, "You're getting better each day. You're going to make it over the top."

Margo knew that before Misty said it. It gets into the bone marrow when a thing becomes that sure. Since they were sounding so good that winning seemed certain, it followed that Margo should ask Miss Preston for permission for them to do a group solo, or quartet presentation, or whatever the program chairman wished to call it. Without using any cuteness she had gotten a firm yes answer. For this she felt very proud.

She listed the name of their group as The Unrelated Siblings. By now they felt like true brothers and sisters—the kind Margo would have liked to have had, all the same age. This meant that no one was ever the middle one. There may have been a time or two when Margo realized that she was getting constant phone calls from boys—Peter and Leroy—that she chose not to think of them as brothers. But the name stood; it was a good one and would lead them to the ultimate success which would call for an ultimate celebration.

"The celebration must follow the recital or be no later than the day after. Peter's folks have gone their limit in letting him finish off the school year, and there's no hope for them extending his time even one more day. We can't possibly celebrate without him," Margo told her friends.

So they all tossed ideas in and out. Far be it from Margo to brag, but she did come up with the perfect idea. And it all happened because her brother grabbed the sports section of the Houston paper and her kid sister grabbed the comics and screeched like mad until Margo let go. The kid could barely read. Margo had turned her back on her true siblings and sat by her father and read the political pages along with him.

"Well, Muffy, what do you think of this? Conroe is getting a new mayor. The mayor they have now is too ill to keep working."

"The new Mayor has Misty's last name. Look! It's her uncle, I know it is. She told us he was going to run for mayor. That's how Misty got the early news about the Halloween parade, remember? She knows all about politics."

Father must have said something in return, but Margo wasn't listening. She was just remembering how Misty's Dundee Scots had saved money and gone to Washington, D.C., and had played for the inaugural of the president of the United States. Besides that, they'd gone on sightseeing trips and eaten in famous restaurants—they had done it all. That's how Margo and her friends would celebrate their big final recital, too—by spending their snake money for a real blow-out! They'd play at the new mayor's inaugural! It was to be June 8. The recital was June 7. Nothing could have been better planned.

After the inaugural, they'd visit Old Town in Spring and buy lots of souvenirs. Then they'd go to Royo's for the best Texas-sized hamburgers ever. If Margo had learned nothing else this year, she'd learned the importance of celebrating properly, of really enjoying her good times. It made her forget the bad times more easily. Of course, she hoped there'd be no bad times at this recital.

But at the next group practice, it began to look like there might be. Misty met them at the door in a blue bathrobe with a towel around her neck; her eyes were puffy. Her grandmother had died. She would be away in Iowa for the next week. She was leaving right after this very practice. An old dented black trunk that must have belonged to her great-great-great-grandparents sat open in the middle of the family-room floor. She had been looking at some old family keepsakes.

"We don't have to practice today," Margo offered. She was almost crying herself, for she loved Misty that much. How can a good friend hurt and you not?

"Absolutely you'll practice! The show must go on. You've practiced in the wind, and you've practiced in the cold, and soon you'll practice in severe heat. There must be no excuses. Just practice, kids. I need to hear your wonderful music."

Margo made her clarinet sound really good for Misty. The others didn't do so badly, either.

Practice time ended at five o'clock sharp as usual. Once they were outside, Margo asked, "Well, what'll we do for practice while Misty's gone for a week?"

Helena said, "Whatever you decide, I'll stick with you, Margo. We are together in this to the finish."

"Yeah," said Peter. "We'll meet at each other's houses and have group practice every day."

Margo nodded. "Our parents will have to cooperate. It's nearing the big recital. They'll understand."

Leroy remained silent.

They looked at him, and finally he said,

"Lately my dad isn't all that interested in me or my drums or anything except a woman named Lillian. It's been that way ever since he fixed her plugged plumbing a month ago. Her little kid flushed a plastic duck down the toilet, only it stuck and did all kinds of water damage because Lillian didn't know there was a shut-off valve just behind the stool."

"Does Lillian like your drum?" asked Margo.

"I think so. She says she does. But people who are in love like everything. I'm not sure."

"Just ask her to come along when your dad brings you over to our houses for practice."

"I think she'll do that much. I think she's that kind of woman, even if she doesn't know about shut-off valves."

Well, Lillian cooperated, all right, though it might not have been such a good idea to involve her. It accelerated the romance. By the end of three weeks, Leroy's dad announced that they'd gotten married. Just like that—no fanfare, no nothing. They'd gone to the justice of the peace and tied the knot.

Margo was livid and told Leroy's dad so. "What an opportunity we missed. We'd have been only too glad to have played for your wedding. It would have been another marvelous rehearsal for the bigtime to chalk up to our credit."

Leroy's dad kiddingly said, "I'll remember that next time."

An even sadder part of all this was that Leroy was moving across town into the house his new stepmother owned. He was now in another school district.

"I guess we can't ask them to get a divorce for the sake of the recital. Everyone's way too happy for that," Margo said.

"Guess not," said Leroy. "I get a big kick out of seeing my new kid brother try my drum. It may not even be legal for me to play in the Fairview recital now."

Peter finally solved it by inviting Leroy to live with him for the remaining six weeks. Since their old addresses had been almost the same anyway, the school would never be the wiser. Leroy's dad said it was a deal if Peter would take his younger son, too, and let him and his new wife have a honeymoon. He was just kidding, again. That's how it is with newlyweds—always happy.

Peter knew it would be okay with his great-grandparents. That's how it was at Peter's, they were always spoiling him rotten. The amazing thing was that it didn't make Peter rotten at all. He and Leroy just became faster friends than ever. In fact, Peter's great-grandparents enjoyed having the whole crew over.

After Misty returned they went back to have her listening ear for their individual practices. But the gang still continued daily group practice. She knew nothing of that or of their planned quartet.

They were keeping their secret from her very well. It was to be their gift to her at the end of the school year.

After one hot, sweaty, summer practice at Peter's, his great-grandparents called Margo's and Helena's parents and asked them to come late. It allowed the kids time to play on a plastic slide down the sloping lawn. The garden crew had watered the grass during the group's practice time.

What a thrill! Margo was having the time of her life. The whole gang was wild with joy. But nobody was enjoying themselves more than Helena. Her mother came early and just stood there watching and smiling. Sometimes Helena would spill over at the end of the run until it looked as if she must be hurt something awful, but up she got and went up that hill again. Margo was squealing and laughing and shouting with the rest.

No one, not even Helena herself, noticed that she had fallen in a strange way on her hand. It wasn't until Helena came to school the next day with a splint on her left pinky that Margo found out she had broken it.

"I can't do my fingering! I won't be able to practice my flute!" she announced sadly.

It looked as if the group had been fatally hit, wiped out by circumstance—with the recital only five weeks away. This was not a matter of getting permission for Peter to stay on, or of Leroy moving in with Peter. They could do nothing about a broken finger.

When they all reported for group practice at Misty's, Helena announced, "This is no excuse, Misty. This is proven by a bona fide X ray."

Misty said, "Well, that's too bad. So let's all practice."

"Helena can't practice," said Margo, not believing.

"I can't practice," agreed Helena.

"How can she practice?" Leroy wanted to know.

"You'd better tell us, Misty. We're not going to guess it," said Peter.

"Helena will play with the fingers that are not broken," explained Misty. "Most of her learning is in her mind, not in her fingers. Helena, you are to listen and *imagine* that you're playing with your pinky, even though you can't move it. Imagine that it is moving. You will attend every single practice and never miss one. No excuses. You'll be healed by the time of the recital, and you'll go onstage as planned."

No one argued with Misty. What she said may have sounded absurd to an outsider. But for insiders who saw the confidence in Misty's face, the conviction and honesty, how could they help but believe her? Margo figured Misty had earned every cent her father had forked over this year, if only for this day alone.

Helena did as she was told. On the day they met at each other's house, she just held her flute with the pinky sticking out in its splint and imagined that she was doing the fingering, imagined her broken pinky moving in place as it should. The boys complained that they missed hearing her usual notes along with their own playing. But Margo insisted that they use *their* imaginations and do what they had to. They did.

The day they came to Margo's house for their last big rehearsal, the one where Helena was actually going to use her pinky, they were greeted by a note from Margo's mother: "Please, dears, practice in the garage. We have company in the guest room sleeping. I've gone to the grocery. Be home soon."

So they practiced in the garage. No hardship could deter them now. The garage was so hot the sheet music was practically scorched, and they were all sweating until their hands were sticking to the wrong places and they thought they'd just die of heat and excitement. But still they practiced on and on and on. One more day. Just one more day, and it would be The Big Recital!

Margo played her full hour, even though she knew her company had to be her grandparents from Illinois. Imagine that! They had gotten her letter and had actually come for the recital! Excitement was building to a grand pitch for everyone. You could even feel it in the air at school.

Was Ernestine excited? Oh yes, and busy practicing, getting very good on her violin. It seemed unfair that Helena, who practiced only inside her head, had to sit next to Ernestine. There was no doubt Ernestine was out for blood. On one dry and brittle dusty day, Margo had found a note scribbled on the trunk of Mother's car. It said, "You better watch out, you better not cry, you're going to get skunked, and that's no lie." It was signed with a drawn star.

Margo knew who the skunk was that had written that. She refused to let it bother her. She felt she was above that petty sort of stuff, and there was nothing in the world that that skunk could do that could shake her one little tiny vibration.

On the day of the recital, everyone had to face an all-school rehearsal in the afternoon. Margo had hidden her clarinet under some posterboard in the music room because she was *that* wary of Ernestine. She and Helena came in just a little early from recess to get their instruments out and ready. Margo felt tense and anxious about breaking this rule, but she was even more tense about being prepared for the recital. What she wasn't prepared for was the total hopelessness she saw in poor Helena's face.

"My instrument has been hijacked!" said Helena. "There's nothing in the case but two slimy snails."

Sure enough, one slimy snail crawled slowly over the top of her case, and another was leaving a slow moist trail along the plush velvet inside.

Ernestine was standing right there in the doorway and said, "Oh, my goodness sakes. First it was music and snakes at the science fair, and now it looks like snails with your music at the recital. Aren't you the creative ones! I should report you."

Margo snapped, "And I hear there are bats in your grandmother's attic, and you're the little witch who goes to entertain them with wild screeching on your violin! Where is it, Ernestine?"

"Don't you come near me. I'll call the principal." Ernestine went running toward the office with Margo in hot pursuit.

The principal was already coming down the hall. He grabbed Ernestine with one hand and Margo with the other and held them directly in front of himself as he squatted just enough to look them square in the eye. "What's this all about?"

"Just teasing," said Ernestine.

He gave her a little push and said, "No teasing. Now—outside where you belong." Then he looked again at Margo and said, "And were you just teasing, too?" She smelled garlic really strong on his breath.

"No, sir, I wasn't teasing at all. Someone has stolen Helena's flute from its case and put two snails inside it. That's hardly a joke on the day of the big recital. You were in the music room just now, weren't you?"

"Uh-uh. How did you know?"

"Miss Preston's garlic dill pickles tempt me, too. But I'm glad to say I resist. Did you see anyone in there fooling around?"

"Well, uh, well a little girl was leaving just before I went in . . . Miss Preston has often offered me a dill pickle, and I sort of felt like having one today. . . ."

"Think hard. Was that girl Ernestine?"

"I guess it was. Just a minute—we'll get Ernestine back in here and settle this."

The principal was six feet four and a half inches tall and had a hand span a mile wide. So Ernestine didn't argue or try to flatter him or anything. She brought Helena's flute out from behind the wastebasket and said, "I told you I was just teasing."

"One more teasing like this, little lady, and we'll have a long serious talk with your parents. Maybe we should report this to Miss Preston right now."

"Oh, please don't do that! She'd bar me from playing my solo in the recital tonight! Please!" Boy, could Ernestine beg!

Margo was surprised to hear herself say,

"Please don't bar her. She's supposed to be the star. She must do her solo."

That surprised Helena, but it put Ernestine into shock. When they got back outside, Helena demanded, "Why? Why did you want to save that—that skunk!" It was the strongest word Helena had ever used.

"How can we know we beat her if she doesn't play?" asked Margo.

"You're right," said her good friend Helena, as a nice wave of garlic smell floated out with her smile. When Margo held her nose, Helena blushed. "You guys took so long, and I didn't know what the principal would do or if I'd ever find my flute, and those pickles were just too tempting," explained Helena.

"Absolutely no excuses are acceptable," said Margo, sounding just like Misty. They laughed.

"I hope everything goes right tonight."

"It will, Helena. Don't worry. Ernestine will know not to try any more tricks. Well, this is our very last practice. Let's make it the best yet, okay?"

"Okay," said Helena, and she turned her thumbs up.

CHAPTER ELEVEN

*I*t did go very well. Once again, Peter was allowed to join them. All four felt things were going their way.

That night, both Margo's grandmothers were at the recital. Her Illinois grandmother helped Margo into the new white silk dress she'd brought for her. She combed Margo's hair a hundred times until it hung like golden silk down the back of her dress. "You look like a little angel, Muffy," whispered her grandmother from Tennessee.

Margo groaned. It was hopeless. She was going to have to listen to things like that the rest of her life, she guessed. But even she liked what she saw in the mirror—except that her face looked awfully pale. She smiled so no one would think for a moment that she was afraid. She wanted to radiate confidence and be a support to her good friends.

Margo was the first of the four to arrive. The high school auditorium was huge. Why didn't her friends hurry? She opened and shut her clarinet case a dozen times.

Leroy and Peter arrived together, of course. Peter was saying, "I'm sweating. I bet I smell like a pig. I wish I wasn't sweating. Why am I sweating when the air conditioner is on?"

"I don't know," said Leroy. "I just feel kinda nervous, like I ought to go out and run a mile. I really want to be good so that my new mother will be proud. She told me this weekend that all three of them are going to be sitting out there listening. You know, this is the very first time she's ever had a kid in a recital. My stepbrother's too young. Dad told me to keep my shirt on this time, as well as my suit coat."

"I won't need your shirt tonight," said Margo, and she laughed nervously. "Gosh, it is hot in here."

Helena was on the stairs by the big stage saying good-bye to her mother and telling her not to worry about a thing. "I've checked my case a hundred times. My flute is in there. My pinky is working fine. I'll do okay. I love you, too."

"Well, the gang's all here!" sang Margo as she opened her case to get out her clarinet.

"My mouthpiece's missing!"

Where? What? Had Ernestine somehow snuck up when she wasn't looking? She retraced her steps. She knew she'd put it in the case before she left home. She was almost sure. Oh gosh, she was done in. Wiped out. Her music days were over.

What could she do? Her friends looked for her, too, even though they were busy, like all the rest, getting their instruments out and ready. The fifth graders went on first. Margo paced back and forth behind the stage. Her blood chilled. She saw someone, a heavy figure flitting past in the shadows of the backdrops. It was Ernestine.

No, it was Peter with his big tuba, bouncing the curtains around. "Margo, Margo! You're too nervous," he said in a deep whisper. The acoustics in this place were something else. "Hold out your hand and count to ten backward. I've got a surprise for you." He placed her mouthpiece in her hand.

"My mouthpiece? Did you take it? That's not funny, Peter."

"I didn't take it. I found it. It had rolled under the curtain and was almost onstage."

"It's mine. Thanks." She said that sort of sullenly. It could still be that Ernestine had somehow snuck it out and tossed it there. On the other hand, maybe she herself, being so nervous, had dropped it somehow in all her checking to make sure her clarinet was still there. She chose to believe Ernestine did it. If she was mad at Ernestine it would help her not be so nervous. And she couldn't afford to be mad at herself right now, just before time to go onstage.

"All sixth graders onstage!"

And suddenly there she was, in the center of bright lights. Her parents and grandparents were hidden out there in the dark audience. *Mustn't let anyone or anything detract. Play before the masses, and you can play anywhere. Think only of music. It doesn't matter if it's a hidden audience or the smell of candy or dill pickles that's driving you wild. Mouthpiece to lips.* Sounds came.

The acoustics were so very good the music soared above and to the sides and behind and surely down front, for the audience was now very silent. Just the beautiful sounds of a sixth-grade band could be heard. It was truly wonderful. At the end of the first number, the applause came up out of the darkness, giving a thrill that surpassed anything.

During Ernestine's solo, Margo looked at her friends. They would be next. Misty was hidden out in that dark audience, too. Wouldn't she be surprised! And they had very well better live up to her belief in them.

Helena was running her fingers, including the pinky that had been broken, up and down her arm as if she were singing "Eency-Weency Spider" in her mind and was carrying out the motions.

Peter's cheeks were puffing in and out, as if he were practicing in his head, too.

Leroy was standing as stiff as a robot with his hands curved rigid and ready for someone to push his *go* button. He had explained to them all yesterday that their piece only took four minutes and that that was but one trillionth of their lifetime if they lived a normal lifespan. He had sounded so brave then, but he was as nervous as any of them now.

At the moment of Ernestine's well-earned applause, Margo thought she might not make it. Then she told herself that she was good, too. She had worked hard to become good, had fought her way to the top, tooth and nail, and had every reason to feel confident. Then miraculously she *was* confident. All that practice and those trial runs had paid off.

With only a glance at each other, the four positioned their instruments and played wonderfully well together.

They were a smash! A real hit. Before three and a half minutes had gone by, Peter's great-grandfather had begun his march up the aisle. And when they finished, he was standing there at the edge of the stage, his arms outstretched. "You did my old tuba proud, Peter!" he said in a voice that cracked a time or two. The crowd heard him and went wild.

Maybe all that applause was for Peter's great-grandfather, but the audience obviously wasn't going to settle down unless someone did something. So what else could Margo do except whisper to the gang to do it again? For their encore, they did their whole four minutes all over again. Then the audience settled down, and the curtains were finally drawn.

Ernestine came at Margo with what seemed like blood in her eyes and death in her heart. Anyway, she made motions as if she were ready to throw the lot of them to the wolves. But Margo was above such ill feelings. She didn't have to be number one; she loved just being a wonderful performer with her group. She smiled at Ernestine and said, "You did very well," and she even said a cheery hello to Ernestine's parents, who agreed that Ernestine was indeed terrific.

Suddenly Margo was able to accept that fact, too, and she said, "Peter will be leaving tomorrow. Would you like to be in our quartet, Ernestine?"

"I am a star, not a part of a group," declared Ernestine.

"You don't know what you're missing," said Margo, accepting the fact that you just can't win with a person like Ernestine. She went out to greet her own family.

Her parents and grandparents all called her sweet names, but mostly they seemed amazed at how well she'd played. Even her brother and kid sister congratulated her. And she felt sort of special to have them as her real siblings. Then she looked around to find the other three of The Unrelated Siblings.

Helena's father was holding Helena's hand, the one that held her flute, high in the air, as if she'd just won some sort of prizefight. Leroy's parents were both hugging him and kissing him as if he were a big part of their love for each other. And Peter's folks weren't worrying about acting dignified at all as they congratulated Peter.

Then there was Misty.

They all got quiet and waited to hear her judgment. She was the best, and she would know. She wouldn't try to flatter them.

"Did we come up even with Ernestine? Did we go to 110 percent?" Margo whispered.

Misty looked very serious as she drawled, "I'd say you did about a 115 percent. You rascals! What a surprise for me—you doing your own special! Ah, you are the best! You deserve a great celebration!"

Margo and crew quickly filled her in about their big plan for that. "Terrific!" sang Misty with a clap of her hands. "My uncle will love to have you at his inaugural. It'll be another rehearsal for the bigtime, and that's where all of you are headed."

Then the cheering started all over again until

Father said it was time for sixth graders to head for home, especially those who had an inaugural to attend the next day. "How about it, Muffy?"

Margo said, "And one day, Father, I'll play for the president of the United States of America, if that's okay with you. I think that trip might be tax deductible."

"Of course it's okay." Father hesitated for a moment and added, "Margo, I'll star that day on my calendar."

Margo, on hearing her real name used by someone in her family, knew she had made it. She was truly number one.